MW01264964

Finishing Life Well

Following the Leadership of Jesus

Published by Kingdom Forerunner Books, Birmingham, Alabama

xulon PRESS

The Finishing Well Series by Paul Hughes.
Finishing Life Well is focused on Christian Discipleship.
Finishing History Well is focused on Christian Eschatology.

Coming in 2013...
Will Cities Finish Well? is focused on the regional transformation Mission of the Church.

www.xulonpress.com
www.kingdomforerunners.com

For Gabriel, Caleb, Daniel, the women who
love them, and their generation.

Table of Contents

The Finishing Well Series

A Simple Request

I never intended to write a book. In April of 2007 I started writing and couldn't stop. It took five years, but what I thought would be one book, became two!

These books grew out of a simple request of Jesus in late February of 2006. I was sitting on a stump in some woods by a stream in Kentucky. I was fasting and praying at the time, when I heard Him whisper in my heart, "Ask Me for anything." It was one of those moments when you feel your whole life could change depending on what happened next. After searching my heart for my greatest desire, I made a simple request.

"I want to finish well."

Life is Short, Eternity Isn't

At fifty-four, I can attest that life is fragile and short. Five months after my simple request, I played several pretty decent full court basketball games in a gym without air conditioning against a bunch of young adults. I crossed up one of my sons at mid-court with a fancy dribble and hit the last shot to win the game for our team. At least that is how I remember it!

The next day, I had a stroke and could have died. The stroke happened in a country with a "stan" at the end of its name and there was no one qualified who could read an image from the one CT scanner within its borders. It didn't look good for me. But I am still here.

Eternity is a heartbeat away. We all live at a time when biblical and historical conditions suggest our generation is moving quickly toward some kind of historic climax. If Jesus doesn't return, we, at the very least, will experience massive global shifts in the coming decades. How should we live? How do we separate what is precious and eternal from what is profane and fleeting?

I want my life and yours to finish well. How we finish our lives is about the heart choices we are making now. Growing in intimacy and obedience with Jesus in grace filled, Spirit empowered, truth centered community is *how* God shapes us for an eternity of glorious partnership with Him. We are all hopelessly flawed, but because of God's great love, we can all receive strength for authentic greatness in this life and beyond.

God made each of us for greatness because He made each of us in His own image. He put us in this world to change it according to His desires expressed through us collectively. That means we must live in constant prayerful conversation to know His heart and operate as His partner in the earth. That is what the Holy Spirit does. He constantly gives us the mind of Jesus! God wants a people who live in the same courageous Holy Spirit as His Son.

Finishing Life Well is about how we can participate now in the Kingdom Jesus is bringing in fullness in the future.

Finishing History Well explores the main biblical views of the End-Times to prepare our generation for what lies ahead.

Will Cities Finishing Well? is about the transformation of cities and regions by the corporate prayers and obedience of the unified Church.

Fixing our eyes

During any historical transition, God's righteousness and Man's sinfulness mature together. The light gets brighter against a darkening sky. Fixing our eyes on Jesus, the leader of the future, will get us through the night. By anyone's standard, the life of Jesus of

Nazareth stands alone in history. No one is more controversial, or compelling. No one is more loved, or hated. If He isn't the God-Man, there is no close second. All my chips are on Him.

Following Jesus' leadership involves creative, redemptive suffering for Him and the values of His Kingdom; but all who give themselves to Jesus inherit a joyful future that cannot be compared.

Therefore we do not lose heart. Though outwardly we are wasting away, yet inwardly we are being renewed day by day. For our light and momentary troubles are achieving for us an eternal glory that far outweighs them all. So we fix our eyes not on what is seen, but on what is unseen, since what is seen is temporary, but what is unseen is eternal. (2 Corinthians 4:16-18)

Let us live well, love well, finish well... and begin again well, under the leadership of our dearest Friend!

Acknowledgments

The Gift of Blurriness

L et me be honest about the voice of my writing in the *Finishing Well Series*. Sometimes I write in a style that appeals to my 25, 22, and 15 year old sons and their friends who hang out at our house. At other times, I write out of the college campus ministry voice in my head which values robust biblical thinking. After thirty years of ministry among college students I have come by that voice honestly. I have wrestled with which audience I am writing to; "Cool dad or serious thinker,… cool dad or serious thinker … cool dad…"

God made me "blurry." That is the word my brother-in-law used after reading a draft of this book … and he is a Bible college president! He said I have the "gift of blurriness." Is blurriness a *gift*?! So, after trying many times to isolate one audience in my head by using one style of writing… I gave up. Seriously. Some chapters are personal and experiential and others are academic and theological. Welcome to my blurry world!

Life is Blurry, but God is Good

Life has a way of moving in and out of focus. Not everything makes sense for more than ten minutes. We all need to find our little life story in the plot of a really big story. Without a bigger story our lives get stuck. For me that big story is the drama of human history and divine romance found in the 66 Books of the Bible.

The grand storyline of the Bible shows we are all on a common journey through time that is really going somewhere. Life and history have a point. Why? Because God is writing the story and He is good!

Therefore, I can look back through the lens of the writers of the 66 Books and make sense out of the blurry legacy of my ancestors. The Bible helps me make sense out of my heart's journey through the blurriness of my generation. Gazing on God, and His storyline for history, anchors me to a hope for the future and for eternity.

A Blurry History

As a Hughes, I come from Scotch-Irish-Welsh pioneers who hacked out a mountain home around 1800 in the Cherokee country of Western North Carolina. My ancestors panned for gold during the rush in North Georgia in the 1830's and helped found towns and churches in Alabama while holding slaves in the 1840's and 50's. They fought for the Confederacy in the Civil War in the 1860's and then stood on the side of racial justice with Dr. Martin Luther King, Jr. in the 1950's. Go figure.

I am the product of a Methodist preacher's home with a strong social justice conscience who got radically born again at age 19. I was powerfully shaped by InterVarsity Christian Fellowship at the University of North Carolina at Chapel Hill. I know what it is like to lead a college Bible study with two dozen students crammed into my dorm room and share the love of Jesus with my drunken Sigma Nu frat brothers and party girls later the same night. As a business major, I took my degree and had a blast in the marketplace world for two years before joining IVCF's full-time campus ministry staff for more than twenty-five incredibly fruitful years. I had LOVED the business world. It felt strange for me to be called a minister.

I am a denominational mutt. Lucy and I have been a part of United Methodist, Presbyterian (PCA), African-American Missionary Baptist, Southern Baptist, and independent charismatic fellowships. I value the drama and beauty of liturgical worship in Catholic, Orthodox, and Anglican traditions. I can speak as an intellectual and also speak in tongues and fall on the floor as a Pentecostal.

I love Jews, Muslims, Hindus, Pagans, and Secular Humanists enough to listen to them, honestly disagree, and try to introduce them to the Jesus I know. I love the smells and ordered chaos of an Uzbekistan Bazaar and I can't wait to get back to Wal-Mart. I can comfortably walk alone across a Black College campus late at night in the "bad part" of town and then sleep in my suburban neighborhood with a pool in our back yard.

I love people. I seek to connect with strangers on their terms in their world, and yet I am haunted by the clear message of the Bible that while we all share the same present, we will not all share the same eternity. A day of judgment is coming and I must warn people I know in a way they understand.

So, I *am* blurry. Hopelessly blurry. Maybe it is because I am wet clay on the Master Potter's wheel just like you. Spinning around, lumps and all, taking shape under the loving pressure of His firm, but gentle hands. Maybe we are *all* blurry, because none of us sees God fully. None of us sees the whole picture of history. None of us can fit every piece of the Bible together.

I have only one non-negotiable in my life. Jesus. He has the last word over all of me. Every thought. Every emotion. Every action. Every relationship. Every decision. He is the one still point in my blurry world.

Many to Thank

There are many who have known Jesus with me whose voices come out in my writing. Some are the voices of lives lived well in the past who still speak in my heart. Dead theologians like Francis Schaeffer and George E. Ladd have helped me write this book. I hope their influences will be word ramps for you toward a greater understanding of "The God Who Is There".

Dr. Jack Arnold was my pastor for eleven years at Covenant Presbyterian Church (PCA) in Winter Park, Florida. Jack and his wife Carol came to faith in Jesus in the home of Bill and Vonette Bright during the early days of Campus Crusade for Christ at UCLA. A classmate of famous author Hal Lindsey, Jack earned a doctorate from Dallas Theological Seminary while winning the top award for Systematic Theology. Over the years, Jack transitioned from Dispensational Theology to Grace Covenant Theology and taught as an adjunct professor at Reformed Theological Seminary in Orlando. His death while preaching in 2005 made national news. Cleartheology.com digitizes 60 of Jack's teaching series and 1200 of his sermons and lessons.

Another of those dead theologians is my Dad, Miles Preston Hughes, Jr. who graduated to Heaven when I was fifteen years old. His 1946 Duke Divinity School thesis, *A Study in the Meaning of Christian Hope in the Epistles of Paul* is remarkable. It is one of those intergenerational batons that I am carrying as I pass it on to the generation coming up behind me.

One of those fast approaching next generation theologians is my oldest son, Gabriel. In many ways I am already following him. As a graduate of Southeastern Bible College and current seminarian at Beeson Divinity School he often pointed me to excellent sources used in these pages. During 2010, Gabriel and several other twenty-something friends planted Hope Culture Church in Birmingham where our whole family worships. I have the privilege of being a senior elder at Hope Culture, but the genius of this amazing expression of church lies in the God of Abraham, Isaac, and Jacob; the God who reveals Himself throughout all generations and desires that all worship Him from an authentic heart.

Our whole family is impacted by the International House of Prayer in Kansas City founded by Mike Bickle. The 24/7 prayer community that began in September of 1999 under Mike's leadership is a sign and wonder in our world today. Mike's associate director is Allen Hood, the President of the IHOP University. Allen is the one who commended my blurriness! He believes my writing weaves biblical concepts into a clearer big picture. You be the judge. Allen is also my brother-in-law and close friend.

National prayer leader and founder of The Call prayer movement, Lou Engle, has also been a major voice in my life. On November 3, 2003 Lou prayed a blessing over me in a dirty downtown warehouse. "God, give this man the desires of his heart for a house of prayer in Birmingham." I am still on that journey, Lou!

Allen Hood, Gary Greene, Jenny Keck, Ed Hackett and I married into the amazing Jack and Beth Downey family and have never been the same! "Poppa D" and "Momma D" sired the culture of the Kingdom into their five kids in a way that is revolutionizing the world. All of their children, their spouses, grandkids, grandkid spouses, and great grandkids, not only love each as best friends, but we all together are best friends with Jesus. In an era when marriage and family is in shambles, we experience a Christ-centered loyalty that covers our many weaknesses as we press on toward knowing the Lord. I have no way of deciphering the untold number of ideas in this book that are the product of family discussions and prayer times.

Though few realize it, the influence of the Eastern North Carolina gentility of my Mom, Helen Prince Hughes Rice, is in my every pore. She still embodies the best of Southern graces where under the broad shady oaks of Dunn, North Carolina she grew up with playmates who knew a simpler world, genuinely more moral than the one today. More than once she tempered my gloomy soap box family room sermons with hope for a better world in the Jesus she knew. I am a better man for it.

It is my Mom's Prince/Hood family tree that I have to thank for the early Pentecostal influences. In 1906 a Holiness preacher named G. B. Cashwell returned to his native Dunn from the famous Azusa Street Revival in Los Angeles. His own January 1907 three week revival in a tobacco warehouse earned him the title "Apostle of Pentecostalism to the South." Cashwell would influence the founders of around a dozen denominations, including the Assemblies of God and the Church of God (Cleveland, TN). His legacy would also influence my Mom's grandparents, Momma and Poppa Hood.

Poppa Hood's booming prayers could be heard outside of the stately Divine Street Methodist Episcopal Church South where he led the Methodist Men. While remaining faithful to Methodism, Momma Hood would often attend the Pentecostal Holiness Church around the corner from Divine Street Methodist. My mother fondly remembers when Poppa and Momma Hood would take her as a girl. to fiery Pentecostal Holy Ghost tent revivals. I cherish that some of the "sawdust trail" sticks to the feet of my ancestors.

I am a huge product of the culture of InterVarsity Christian Fellowship. Many of the stellar people I have known in ministry have been a part of the IVCF family. There are far too many former students and ministry colleagues for me to acknowledge here, but I do want to single out Bruce Alwood. Bruce, you patiently supervised me through the years of transition from campus work to the founding of a whole new ministry. This writing project began during my nine month ministry sabbatical of 2007. How grateful I am for InterVarsity's pastoral culture which helps people exiting employment to transition well. Bruce, you did it for me, man!

I am grateful to Pastor Bart Brookins and the faith family at Fullness Christian Fellowship who loved my family well while books were written, Kingdom Forerunners was launched, and Hope Culture Church was birthed. It is churches like Fullness that are helping Birmingham become the city of Jesus' dreams.

The Birmingham Prayer Furnace is indebted to other local churches, like Metro Church of God while under Mark Schrade, and Living Church Ministries under Bishop Demetrics and Pauline Roscoe. I am also grateful for ministries with city-wide vision like The Lovelady Center under Brenda Spahn, Joshua Generation under Jody Trautwein, Love Well Ministries under Lestley Drake, the Metro Birmingham Evangelical Ministers Association under Jack Eyer, prayer leadership partners like Kevin Moore with Mission Birmingham, Mark Miller with the Greater Birmingham Annual Mayor's Prayer Breakfast, and Birmingham Police Chief A.C. Roper with Prayer Force United.

At the state level, I am grateful for the inspirational leadership of Kyle Searcy, Director of the Alabama Alliance of Reformation and Pastor of Fresh Anointing House of Worship in Montgomery. It is an honor for Lucy and me to be ordained under his pastoral authority. Brother, Kyle, because of men of God like you, incredible things are ahead for the Body of Christ in Alabama!

I am grateful for those I share the long journey with for restoring honor to Native Americans; Dale Cathey with Servants of Christ, Tom Dooley of Pathclearers, Cherokee leader Randy Woodley, Muscogee Creek minister Melba Checote Eads, Yuchi leader Negiel Bigpond, and Inuit leader Suuquina. Justice is coming.

Internationally, the Birmingham Prayer Furnace and the Campus Prayer Networks are deeply influenced by the values of our friends Pete Grieg, David Blackwell, Nathan and Marisa Chud, Ryan and Allison Riggs, and others with the 24/7 Prayer and Boiler Room communities. Thanks blokes!

To the Kingdom Forerunners board; wow. What a journey God has us on! Al and Danielle, John and Cindy, Brett and Kenzie, Lucy and I can't imagine dreaming these impossible dreams for God's Kingdom to come on earth through 24/7 prayer, justice, and mission with anyone else! You guys believe in the vision when no one else has a clue. Your voices in my life keep me believing, too.

Thanks to Kingdom Forerunners staff and former staff Gabriel Hughes, Ike Ubasineke, Pierre Blackman, Jared Fonseca, Erica Jackson, Natalie Farber, Tim and Ericka Frye, Matt Makar, Adrienne Scott, Jeff Davis, Kelly Curtler, Sherei Jackson, Emily Day, Brent McGough, Carly Downey, Clayton Mullins, Jana Laher, Taylor Webb, Matt and Holly Hobson, and the many volunteer singers, musicians, and intercessors filling the bowls of prayer in Heaven from out of the Birmingham Prayer Furnace! Nothing happens without prayer! May these books find their way into your hands and hearts to better fashion prayers of faith that prepare us, our families, our city, our region, and this global generation for the leadership of Jesus.

Finally, no one, other than Jesus, deserves more gratitude or has more claim of influence on me than my wife, Lucy. Honey, it is your life that has helped me to best know the one Voice that matters most. I have done the writing, but you have done the loving that made it possible. You hear the urgency of our moment in history when others do not. Many things are blurry around us, but Sweetheart, with one certain voice we stand as a man and woman together with our three amazing sons (and the women who love them) to declare to all who are listening... Jesus is coming. People get ready.

Finishing Life Well

Part One

Beginning With the End in Mind

Chapter 1

Learning to Trust the Heart of Jesus

*"Philip said, "Lord, show us the Father and that will be
enough for us." Jesus answered, 'Don't you know me,
Philip, even after I have been among you such a long time?
Anyone who has seen Me has seen the Father.'"*
(John 14:8-9)

Where Do We Begin?

Where does one start a book about finishing life well? At the end of course!

We may disagree on the particulars, but I believe every human being has a common destiny.

Some would say we all simply cease to exist. From dust we came, to dust we return. Period. It was nice while it lasted.

Some would say we all get to Heaven. (Insert your definition of heaven here.) All roads lead to the top of the mountain. Your road is just as good as my road. See you at the top!

Some would say that you have to search with all your heart to find the one narrow gate which leads to the Celestial City. That would be me. Actually that would be me borrowing an image from John Bunyan, who wrote an old book called *The Pilgrim's Progress*.

Some just never stop to think much about it. Life can be so cruel and so confusing that the thought of how to finish life well just never gets examined closely. But there is a finish line all the same.

Some people don't accept the idea there is one reality we are all sharing. Somehow we are living in separate universes and the discussion of common destiny is irrelevant.

I am not going to beat around the bush here. I believe something. You do not have to agree with my belief, but if you are going to read this book, here is where you decide whether to invest your precious time and energy with my thoughts or do something far more interesting in the postmodern carnival of life.

I believe every human being will stand before a man most people alive today have heard about in some fashion - Jesus. There you have it.

Okay! For those of you still reading, I will sum up the 66 books of the Bible; the first place to learn more about this man, Jesus.

Bible 101

God creates world. God creates Man male and female to govern the world He just made. Some creepy competitor fakes the first Mom and Dad out. They blow it big time. God knew this would happen and begins revealing an insanely ingenious way to make everything right again. Yada, yada, yada. You and I get born somewhere in this process.

Oh, I left out the part where this Jewish carpenter guy from Smallville, gets a Messiah complex and dies for the sins of the whole world. Only he really IS the Messiah and he really *did* take away the sin of the world in the freakiest way you can imagine. He died nailed to a big stick and then angels busted Him out of His grave. He left some followers who really didn't know what in the world to do except sit in a room and pray night and day until something happened.

Something happened.

From the streets of the most fought over city on the planet a message began to sound. That same message is still ringing in our ears today. One of Jesus' buddies named Pete was the first guy to belt it out and it goes something like this:

"Hey everybody! I know y'all are all here to party and have a good time in Jerusalem this week. But God has a major news flash and a bunch of us just got hammered with His Happy Bomb and can't help ourselves. We have to tell you something, or we will explode!

"Remember that Jesus guy who got killed a couple of months back? You know the one? Oh yeah! He was basically God and we killed him. Well, actually He chose to be killed to pay for all of our screw-ups as part of a deal that He had worked out with His Dad before they made the universe together. Wild, huh?!

"It's kind of an amnesty deal, where only the people who know they are guilty as sin get included. That makes the whole world eligible, beginning with you guys!

"But anyway! Because He died and is alive again, anybody who wants to believe this amazing news and join us crazies who hung out with Him a lot before, and after, He died, can live in the future government He is coming back to set up!

"Sign-up sheets are by the pool after we hear your confession and dip you in the water to welcome you into this new community. Any takers?! Sweet."

Fast forward about 2000 years. Throw in scandals, holy wars, revivals, justice movements, heroes and zeros, and... we are still waiting for Jesus to step in to this mess of human history and make something ridiculously pure and eternal out of it.

Will We Finish Life Well?

You may be tempted to detect a note of cynicism. Don't. After 2000 years this Jesus thing is still the deal. Sure, the institution that formed during the first few generations after he took up temporary residence in Heaven is divided, full of messed up people, and is sometimes an embarrassment to His reputation.

I believe it isn't that the Jesus Way has been tried and found wanting, it is that the Jesus Way has most often not been tried. Or maybe we have the wrong idea of what is supposed to happen when we do follow Him and we aren't rich, famous, or healthy. Maybe His Kingdom is different from the way the world, and a lot of churches, measure kingdoms. Just maybe.

People in every generation, from realists to dreamers, who have searched under every rock they can find for truth and reality, keep finding their way to this naked, grossly twisted, bloody man who was nailed on a tree with spit on his face. Somehow, in the futility of that horrible scene, the shame that is our own and the glory that is God's, wrecks our souls without remedy. Bam.

I am one of those. I can't shake this Jesus guy. I can't make Him just go away. He is not a flash in my pan. He isn't yesterday's news. For me, He is today's news. And tomorrow's news. I have looked at every other lover and religion I can find. But when I am most honest, my heart says, "Paul, no one loves you better than this Man."

I have never seen Jesus! But I love Him. I talk to him all the time. But I have never heard his voice outside of my own heart. It's crazy. I'm crazy. But I can't live any other way. I am in love with an invisible King. I am betting my life on a guy who spoke Aramaic, a language I will never speak. He wasn't trained in seminary. He wasn't even a successful leader, unless showing his followers the best way to get in trouble and risk death for the sake of love and truth is concerned. He ticked-off a whole bunch of powerful people off during his three and half year campaign of declaring a Kingdom that isn't like any other. Few people including his closest friends really "got him". This is the Messiah? C'mon. But I can't help believing that He *is*.

Don't read the stories about Jesus and try to water down his outrageous claims to deserve the total loyalty of every living person. "If anyone comes to me and does not hate his father and mother, his wife and children, his brothers and sisters – yes even his own life- he cannot be my follower." He actually said that. What do we *do* with a statement like that?! How do we respond to a human being who *makes* a statement like that? Clearly, Jesus was forcing the Messiah issue in His generation. Was He the One they were looking for or not? That was then. What about now?

This is my take. He is just as jealous for you and me to come face to face with the same hard reality today. Jesus is saying the same thing to you and me that He did to the Roman and Jewish authorities of His day, "I am large and in charge. Deal with it."

That is maybe what we might expect a God-Man to say. But then He says things like (and I paraphrase), "All who are tired of the weight of life, come and hang out with me. Get into partnership with me. Let's do life together and then you will discover that though I am the strongest, coolest Man who ever lived, I am the most gentle and humble, too. I will choose weakness, just to be with you forever, because I want to convince your heart over and over that I really am good and love you better than any other. You are going to need to know that, because before the end of the day, you will be hated on my account. Are you with me?" (Matthew 11:28-9, John 13:3-7)

If the destiny of every human being is exactly that; to stand before this red hot Lover who is also the Leader of the Universe, then what are we doing!? Will we finish life well as individuals? Will we finish our collective planetary life story well, too?

Remember Me!

If there is any hope for us, as sons and daughters of Adam and Eve, it does not lie in our common past. We messed that one up. It doesn't lie in a really awesome leader who can unify the world under the spirit of this Age. Someone like that is coming, but that leader will hate the Living God and be the product of all our human generated independence and corruption. My hope for a happy ending and "world peace" lies in a common future under one leader who has already come. He waits in Heaven to come again. The Bible isn't fuzzy on the identity of who that world leader is.

The good news for you and me is that our hope for an eternal future of amazing joy is not dependent on where we start. Ask the guy who was being crucified next to Jesus outside the Jerusalem gate. That man was a thief who came to realize even as he was *ridiculing* Jesus that He was indeed the One sent to save the world. This thug changed his mind right there on the cross and cried out, "Remember me, Jesus, when you come into your Kingdom."

Jesus looked through His blood-blurred vision into the eyes of His cross mate and welcomed His newest friend with these words. "Today you will be with me in Paradise!" (Luke 23:42-42)

27

Jesus wants weak, broken lovers to do life with Him forever. My goal is to hear Jesus say words like these to me: "Paul, I want to do eternity with *you*. I don't hold anything in your past against you! Come on! An eternal "Universe 2.0" of dynamic partnership in a beloved community awaits us together!"

You can start poorly and end well. You can start well and end poorly. It all depends on the nature of your personal conversation with God. If there a "yes", even a weak "yes" at the core of your heart to trust Jesus, you are on the right track.

Chapter 2

How Fear and Desire Shape Our Life Story

"The end of a matter is better than its beginning." (Eccl. 7:8)

*"Fear God and keep His commandments...for God will
bring every deed into judgment, including every hidden
thing, whether it is good or evil."* (Eccl. 12:13-14)

Solomon's Story

There is deep irony in the above sayings of Solomon, King of
Israel. Maybe he learned the wisdom of ending well from his
many mistakes in life. He, like so many people in the Bible, finished
poorly. Issues of sexuality, stewardship of money and resources, and
unmerciful treatment of others tripped him up. It is sobering to think
about.

Everybody starts life somewhere. Some of us start life with a
silver spoon in our mouths as the old folks say. Born into privilege.
Others start life with a boot on their neck. Born into oppression.
Some start life with a full playing deck of talent. Others start life "a
few pickles shy of a barrel" according to Jed Clampett, a hillbilly
who lived in Beverly Hills.

If you are reading this book, I want to say, "Congratulations!
You made it this far!" Life, no matter what the circumstances, is a
gift. In spite of how hard the knocks and how often they come, it is
a gift. You can't finish well if you don't begin some place and are

still somewhere along the way. No matter how horrible today was, tomorrow will come with a fresh package of amazing grace with your name on it. Starting well is good, finishing well is better. If you are alive, you still have a shot.

Solomon wrote three of the 66 books in the library better known as the Bible. He started REALLY well ... sort of. His father's first contact with his mother Bathsheba, was a forced sexual encounter, that would be classified today as rape. Only the rapist happened to be the King of Israel who watched Solomon's mom bathing in eye-shot of the palace balcony and decided he would abuse his power to get her. This is the part of the video we skip over at my house to get to the next scene.

Though Solomon was a half-illegitimate child, the favor of God was on him from birth. He had something in common with Jed the Hillbilly. Solomon was nicknamed "Jedidiah" which means "loved by the Lord." He is eventually chosen to rule the Kingdom with a pile of money. This did not endear him to his siblings. His Dad makes the decision to make Solomon his successor while pretty much on his death bed with a young virgin that the doctors gave him as an electric blanket. If David didn't make a move on this girl, as demonstrated by his taking so many other wives, then he must have been near death!

Did I mention that Solomon's adulterous father had a hit put out on his Mom's former husband to cover up the affair? I wonder how Solomon felt about *those* facts growing up? Did the other kids around the palace playground remind him of that old headline in the Jerusalem Gazette?

I am not making this stuff up! If you thought the Bible was boring, you probably haven't read it enough or with the imagination God gave you. Why would God put sordid life stories, like this one, in *His* story? Why would God's people write about their own kings' failings so honestly for countless generations to read?

Maybe it is because it is our story, too. I don't know the circum-stances of your birth. Maybe you do. Or maybe you don't. But God does. He knew you in your mother's womb. He knew your mother in her mother's womb. He knows the hidden and shameful parts of you and your family history and it doesn't scare him off. I heard a preacher say something once that stuck with me. "The only thing we add to our salvation, is the sin that makes it necessary."

After trying to understand everything I can about God, the world, and myself, I keep coming back to the central message of the Bible. I am hopelessly flawed, and deeply loved.

I come from a pretty cool family legacy. You will hear some of it in these pages. I am too smug about it at times, because I really consider many of my ancestors and relatives amazing people. I have a family reputation to live up to and real heroes to imitate. But thank God, maybe like Solomon, I haven't forgotten the deep pain, the shameful chapters, and the choices to forgive and be forgiven along the way that have enabled God to keep shining his face on me and my kin.

A Good Beginning

Solomon, as a teenager, wins the Powerball lottery of the ancient Middle East. Riches, power, youth. Whoa. Where is this going?

God comes to him in a dream as Solomon starts his reign and they have a conversation. This was no ordinary dream. There are "pizza dreams" and then there are dreams like Solomon's, or Isaac's son, Jacob's, who saw God at the top of a stairway to heaven. Some of you may not have realized that the Stairway to Heaven was more than just a classic 70's rock tune you can download on your iPhone.

In Solomon's dream, he gets to ask God for one thing. It is like finding a magic lamp with two of the three wishes already used. So what did he ask for? Wisdom.

He knew that he did not know much. He understood that he did not have understanding. He was weak and young and he felt his frailty and vulnerability and he was afraid of really messing-up those things that his Dad had worked all his life to arrange. There were plans for a really awesome national prayer room to be built, there were people to govern, and there were other nations around that might think that with David, the giant slayer, gone, now would be a good time to test the boundaries with his punk son in charge.

The Role of Fear

Fear, in one sense, is a very good thing. God gave us emotions so we could perceive things in a way beyond mere logic and observation. Fear is motivating. Who we are, and what we become in life, is a function of what we fear and what we desire.

My family liked to camp when I was a child. I can't remember staying in a hotel until a fraternity pledge trip in college! On one camping trip in the Smoky Mountains, a large black bear came to breakfast. I was a baby. I couldn't even toddle. I had not yet developed a sense of fear of large black, hungry, forest animals. But my Dad and Mom and two brothers and two sisters had gone before me in the fear and knowledge realm.

Therefore, instead of leisurely discussing the relative merits of sharing the delicious bacon and eggs off the Coleman stove with one of God's good creatures, they fled to the car. Fortunately for me, my mother grabbed me before making the trip. My baby flesh might not have been more interesting for the bear to taste than the bacon, but who knows! My mother's fear of the bear, and love for me, allowed me to see another day. Thanks, Mom.

Solomon begins his collection of proverbs saying, "The fear of the Lord is the beginning of knowledge, but fools despise wisdom and discipline". (Proverbs 1:7)

Solomon sums up his second book of wisdom, called Ecclesiastes (meaning the Teacher of the assembly), this way. My paraphrase is, "Do you want to live well and finish well? Fear God and do what He says, because His evaluation of your life at the end of the day is the only one that counts!" Fear has a dark side, too. It isn't *the* Dark Side. ("Luke, I am your Father.") But it can escort you there.

We must all learn to face, manage, overcome, or deal with the fears in our life. It is the reason armies train soldiers under realistic combat situations and weed out all but the most resilient. It is also the reason armies historically have shot men who break ranks and run from the enemy. Fear can spread. But so can faith and courage.

Sometimes, we are in situations where fear is the only option. A hierarchy of fears in our own hearts determines our actions. Do I charge into the wrath of the enemy or do I take a chance that my own leader will kill me? A fear of radical Islam's version of God is also the reason that some people strap on bombs or fly passenger planes into buildings and blow themselves up along with other people. Choose your fears and your God wisely.

Solomon's healthy fear of failure escorted him into the wisdom of God. He felt a need for wisdom from God above everything else. He was not wise in his own estimation.

One Thing

How about you? If you could ask God for just one thing, what one thing would you ask Him for right now? Do you have your life figured out? Is it all set in order in your iPhone?

You might be saying, "That's easy, he just gave us the right answer. Duh, wisdom." Not so fast. Be honest with God and your own heart.

I ask people a particular question pretty often. They are usually people I am meeting for the first time. "What one thing would you like for Jesus to do for you right now?" Because I live in the heart of the Southern United States, a.k.a. the Bible Belt, I can get away with this question. People around where I live tend to think Jesus is pretty cool and is probably God, so it works.

It amazes me that people normally do not flinch when I ask them this. As you might predict, the thing most on their hearts is healing for a loved one, a material dream to come true, passing a test, or something temporal. In a hundred years or a day it probably won't matter that much.

The Role of Desire

Like our fears, what we desire reveals a great deal about who we are and what we are becoming. Fear and Desire are actually two sides of the same coin.

If I am afraid of writing this book (and I am) then it is because I desire not to appear like a complete idiot to everyone who reads it. And, I really don't like conflict and there is a pretty good chance that I will say something that will make somebody mad. And, I can't lie to save my life and I will probably write something terribly embarrassing that my grandchildren will hate me for. And, even though people tell me I am a great writer and ought to write a book, I really don't like writing and everything in the world has already been said a gajillion times already. And, ... you get the picture.

But I also have these faint desires. What if I really have something to say that might actually help someone? That would be cool. What if somewhere along the way, I actually begin to enjoy writing more than checking sports scores on the internet? Sweet.

What if God actually wants me to write and I would be disobedient to His good pleasure in making me out of dust? Okay, that one is a mixture of fear *and* desire! But that is my point. I want things that terrify me. That is why I am a member of the human race. We are filled with fears and desires and they are all mixed together. We fear what we desire and desire what we fear.

That is why war, suspense, comedy, romance, and horror films, (which I personally only fear) will always be the stuff of good movies. We are so dang conflicted and we can't help it! We pay good money and waste good time to see other people in situations just like ours or far worse.

But let me take it up a notch or two. To passionately desire God, the most terrifyingly beautiful, powerful, and yet most gentle being of all, is the highest pursuit of the human heart. Movies only stir the innate sense of eternity that God Himself has placed inside every human breast.

How do we get on the right path that will lead us to encounters with our Maker, Leader, Lover, Bridegroom, Judge, and Friend? One way is to interrogate your own soul under the bright lamp of your highest longing.

The Question

So what do YOU want Jesus to do for YOU right now? For real. (Start the Jeopardy thinking jingle now.)

I like it when people recognize that I am not kidding or looking for a way to tell them the right answer. If they tell me what they want, I offer to say a prayer on the spot to agree with them for what they are asking Jesus to do in their lives. Maybe He will do it! Maybe I am just the excuse they were looking for to put something on the asking table and God in His kindness really wants to bless them just as they asked.

But I have to admit, there was this one time at a Church's Chicken in Memphis where the guy cleaning the floor kept giving me answers that I couldn't agree with for him. After he gave me the "big house" answer, and the "million dollars in the bank" answer, I decided to help him along to something better. I felt like he was asking, not too high, but too low.

Finally, he stopped trying to figure out what this White guy in the Black community was really looking for, besides the fried okra, and he asked *me* what *I* would ask Jesus for.

If you already have Jesus and He has you, maybe it's okay to ask for a bigger crib and more bling. Maybe. Maybe not. But if life is short and eternity isn't, we need to mostly desire the things that will still be there after the body is cold. Maybe life is about more than "Get rich or die trying" which is the message of the Gang and Prison Rap music culture.

Maybe the real issue of my acquaintance's heart at Church's Chicken was gaining a way out of the violence, hopelessness, and powerlessness of his neighborhood. I needed to hear that, too, and not judge a brother by the rules of my neighborhood.

But I was willing to bank on something else in that moment. I was willing to believe that in spite of cultural, racial, and economic differences, God had made us both with fears and desires that could only be met in encounter with Himself. He had set eternity in both our hearts and whether the dirt He used to make us was red Georgia clay, black Mississippi mud, white Florida beach sand, or brown like the dirt in my back yard in Birmingham, we were still dirt with an eternal destiny in the heart of our Dad.

I told him that day, that if I could ask Jesus for just one thing, I would ask to know Him as fully as He knows me. I told that dear man my honest answer that day. Deep intimacy with God is what I desired above everything else. He seemed to buy it. At least he had figured me out, if nothing else.

The Food Chain of Passions

Fear can escort us into wisdom, if fear of the One revealed in the Bible is at the top of our fear food chain. Desire can escort us into life's highest pleasures, if our greatest passion is to know Jesus intimately and please the glad heart of our Awesome Dad in Heaven.

It isn't that we are creatures without desires and fears. We are creatures with fears and desires that are too small, or we have the wrong passions altogether. Who we are, and who we are becoming, is revealed plainly by our gut level fears and desires. Where we spend eternity is less about God judging us in the future than it is about the reality of our own hearts, *now*.

Chapter 3

Developing a "One Thing" Desire

"One thing I ask of the LORD, this is what I seek:
that I may dwell in the house of the LORD all the days of my life,
to gaze upon the beauty of the LORD
and to seek him in his temple."
(Psalm 7:4)

What David Discovered

If Solomon's dad, King David, had been with me at Church's Chicken, he would have told the young man his highest desire in the verse above. Gazing at the Beautiful God forever!

David was a very passionate man. He wrote many songs, he fought countless battles, he loved lots of women. But David's greatest desire was to be near the Holy One of Israel and gaze on His shining glory 24/7 over the Ark of the Covenant. He was so daring in his desire to gaze on the beauty of God's presence that he risked his life to put the Ark in a tent that was open for all worshippers to look at. He lavishly spent Israel's treasury to commission teams of singing priests, prophets, and musicians to worship and pray night and day before the Lord.

David sought God's heart out of his highest desire. But the unvarnished Bible story reports the horrible adultery with Bathsheba and murder of her husband Uriah a few chapters *after* David established the open worship of God in Zion.

David may have grown to love the heights of God's glory during his successes in life, but it was during his darkest failures that David found the depth of God's mercy. Killing a really, really big evil man with nothing but a sling and a little rock in front of two whole armies as a teenager is a pretty heady experience; but killing a good man, a faithful servant and friend, just so you can have his wife, that is the kind of thing you think about killing *yourself* about.

David discovered something more in the heart of God in the place of utter failure than he could have found anywhere else. He found unconditional mercy for all who confess their brokenness. He found in the God of Abraham, of Jacob, of Moses, what Biblical Greek calls, "agape", or, "just because" love.

David discovered a universal reality about God's heart. *All* who call out of the true poverty of their own heart to this God of mercy *will* be rescued. For all His awesome, majestic being and power, the God of David has one weakness. He cannot resist a humble heart. David discovered a desire in God that trumps any desire to bring judgment. God *delights* to show mercy! That discovery will drive you back to gaze at His beauty!

Finding God's Heart of Mercy

God doesn't just tolerate giving us mercy because He *has* to do it as part of His Heavenly job description. My preacher brother-in-law, Allen Hood, peers into the warped psychology of our human soul when we fall short of pleasing God and exposes a dialog that goes something like this: "I've screwed up again. Oh well. It is a good thing that God is a God of mercy. He has to forgive me because there is that clause about how Gods of Mercy have to forgive us when we ask for it. I know He really doesn't *like* forgiving me, but He died for me on the cross and now He is stuck with me."

NO! We have no concept of the depth of God's delight in showing us mercy, because we do not grasp the goal of His passion for intimacy with us. He is after a voluntary love response in our hearts towards Himself. Those who have been forgiven much, love much. Experiencing the limitless depth of His mercy guides our hearts into the ocean of His love and a more authentic personal relationship! He really is like this! He really is this kind and this good! He loves to give us mercy so that we can know His heart and the depth of His passions!

Can it be true? "Amazing love, how can it be, that Thou my God hast died for me!?" Charles Wesley put these words to song in the midst of the early Methodist movement. The wound of this kind of boundless love casts out all our fears and other loves. No one loves *you* more than this Man in whom God dwells fully—Jesus.

If you have never failed and known true guilt and shame, you do not know what David found out. Even secular psychologists have learned that in order to become a healthy, mature human being, one must experience true forgiveness for true guilt. Freely given "in-spite of" relationship is the Truth that sets us free. It isn't the truth of our sin that sets us free, though acknowledging the cold hard facts is a step in the right direction. It is the truth we have sinned and that the relentless heart of God is *unfazed by us* that sets us free. He *will* remove everything that hinders the free flow of affection between our hearts and His. Our part is to let Him love us.

Even though God in no uncertain terms told David through a prophet friend that the son of the adultery would die because "you have shown utter contempt for the Lord," David pleaded with God for the life of the child with prayer and fasting for seven days. The passion with which David pursued God's heart to be merciful in spite of the direct prophetic word stunned those around him. After the child died his servants asked, "Why did you act this way?" David's reply gives us insight into His relationship with God:

While the child was still alive, I fasted and wept. I thought, "Who knows? The Lord may be gracious to me and let the child live." (2 Sam. 12:22)

The Divine "Who Knows?!"

I don't know what you have done or how bad the consequences of it. Was there trouble in David's life and family because of the character flaws in his life? Oh yeah! God is not mocked. If you do cruddy things, cruddy things will happen to you. Read what God said would happen to David in 2 Samuel 12:10-12 for a real eye-opener on that point. But that did not keep David from betting on God's desire to show mercy all of his life.

There is a divine, "Who knows?!" emblazoned over your life as well. Maybe, just maybe, God will be impacted by your genuine repentant and broken heart and empower you to finish your life well as He longs for you to do.

At the end of it all, David understood that his incredible acts of obedience, wonderful as they were, could not save the day. There were also too many acts of "utter contempt for the Lord." If the God of his fathers was to be his God, too, he would have to know Him for himself in the place of greatest weakness and absolute brokenness. David wrote a song that went like this:

Where can I go from your Spirit? Where can I flee from Your presence? If I go up to the heavens, You are there; if I make my bed in the depths, You are there. If I rise on the wings of the dawn, if I settle on the far side of the sea, even there Your hand will guide me, Your right hand will hold me fast. If I say, 'Surely the darkness will hide me and the light become night around me,' even the darkness will not be dark to You; the night will shine like the day, for darkness is as light to You. (Ps. 139:7, 11-12)

God is there in all seasons and situations in life. If we only reach out to Him as humbly as we know how, He *will* do the rest. David was a mess. But he received God's love at the lowest point of his life, because he *knew* that God would always have mercy on a humble, broken heart. David's very name means "Beloved". It is your name, too! Finishing well is not about a perfect track record. It is about never quitting on a God, who will never quit on us.

We are talking about a God who became a Man and died on a Roman cross outside a Jewish city to prove his commitment to thoroughly love all from any generation and culture who would receive Him. No other religious system, prophet, book, or even the institution of the historic church itself can undo the zeal in God's heart to finish well what He has started in you.

Chapter 4

God is a Lover

"How great is the love the Father has lavished on us, that
we should be called children of God!"
(1 John 3:1)

What Judas Missed

I could be wrong, but I believe that if Judas, the friend of Jesus who betrayed him, had not given up on himself for just three more days, the same Man he betrayed with a kiss in the garden, would have kissed Judas again after His resurrection in the Upper Room.

Judas's sin was no greater on one level than David's, but Judas missed the heart of God and killed himself. He never knew the real heart of the Man he saw heal the sick, raise the dead, and eat with outcasts. When we miss the emotions of this God- Man Jesus, we will never know that He can carry us in His heart far beyond where our own heart can ever go, if we let Him. The sober message of Judas' life is this: we can be around Jesus and never *really* know Him. I fear that is the vast condition of our generation.

A Hunk of Burning Love

Solomon also took up songwriting like his dad. His third book is called "Song of Songs". He wrote it for his Shulamite bride.

For Love is as strong as death, its jealousy unyielding as the grave. It burns like blazing fire, like a mighty flame. Many waters cannot wash it away. If one were to give all the wealth of his house for love, it would be utterly scorned. (Song of Songs 8:6-7)

The Beatles sang, "Money can't buy me love!" They were right, too. The currency of Heaven that "buys" God's love is a lovesick heart longing for Him.

The Song of Songs by Solomon is one doozey in the 66 books. It is a not-so-thinly veiled account of sexual encounter and romantic play between husband and wife. It has commonly been understood as a metaphor of God's passion and zeal for his Bridal People Israel of old and the Bride of Jesus today. It was steamy enough to be debated by leaders in Israel as to whether it should be included in the Bible. Aren't you glad they did!

God is a red-hot lover and make no mistake about it. He is the original "hunk-a-hunk-a burning love" that Elvis Pressley sang about. Maybe only Elvis could get away with making a song as absolutely corny as "Burning Love" a hit. But when God revealed Himself as a consuming fire to the nation of Israel in the desert it was anything but corny. After bringing them out of slavery in Egypt with miracles that are stupefying the world to this day, it was to bring them to Sinai for a marriage covenant ceremony that went something like this:

You are My treasured possession, the apple of My eye, and all My delight is in you! I have plans for you that you have no ability right now to even comprehend. If you learn to trust Me and My love for you, then there is no limit to how much joy and blessing I will pour out on you in front of every other people in the earth. I will dwell in your midst in My beauty and awesomeness. When you call to Me, I will answer. I will provide for you 24-7. I will fight your battles for you and I will guarantee your future forever. (My paraphrase of Ex. 19:5-6)

You didn't have to be a prophet to hear these words. Jewish Rabbis today teach that even the lowliest of Israel's maidservants "saw" the Holy One of Israel, the One God of Heaven and Earth, dwelling in fire and smoke on the mountain that day.

As Yahweh first spoke to Moses out of a burning bush, He now spoke to the whole nation of Israel from a burning mountain. Sinai was the same mountain where He first did the burning bush thing with Moses. But it was a bigger crowd this time. About 2.5 million people in fact. Men, women, and children, who really weren't used to camping out and to whom Egypt wasn't looking so bad anymore.

Yahweh's audible voice was so loud, like a ram's horn from heaven, that it absolutely terrified the people. They asked Him not to hear His voice like that anymore. *"Moses, it would be just okay with us, if you go up to the top of the mountain, behind the cloud, to meet with Yahweh, but we will keep our distance. You tell us what He wants, thank you very much."* (My paraphrase of Ex. 20:18-21) In His relative tenderness, Yahweh, was still overwhelming to his own covenant people. He hid Himself from their sight with fire and smoke, but that was still too much for them to handle. It is a tragic scene that describes every generation down to our day. God is great and we really do not want to know Him as He really is. Jesus said it this way, *"This is the verdict: light has come into the world, but men loved darkness more than light because their deeds were evil."* John 3:19 Jesus *knew* we would kill Him, but that did not stop Him from loving us to the end.

When our first Mom and Dad were sent away from the visible presence of their Maker, we all as their offspring lost the very capacity to stay in a sustained encounter with God. We were all there inside their bodies that day when they broke faith with God. We lost the ability in us to know Him face to face as they did. We, like our first parents, are naked and ashamed and we hide from God. He is light and we love darkness more than we love Him. It hurts to live in His light, because we are so corrupt.

We Have Issues

Hopefully, you agree with me that the human race has some major issues. Of all the beliefs taught in the Bible, the one that can be most thoroughly proven empirically is that every person has issues, a.k.a. sin. Big, black, gnarly sin. Sin isn't just what you did last night, it is your nature. Like a bent arrow aimed at a target, you will always miss the mark; every time. Falling short, missing the mark, sin. It is our common human condition whether we acknowledge it or not. But missing the mark is more than our inability to fly straight. We aim for the wrong target. We are all under a death sentence. What if there is no outside help, no Messiah? Human history will not get resolved through better technology, or a humanistic one world government where we just all get along. Don't hold your breath for utopia in this present age. If you don't know this, I can't help you!

We have "bent-ness" in all of us. We can't finish well anymore, because we can't even start well. I must have "straight-ness" to fly to the bulls-eye, but our bent-ness is always in us. On my best days, there is still something that Jesus had to die for on the cross. This actually really upsets me... in a good way. The more I understand I can never save myself, the more I live the way Jesus wants me to live. I will *never* get to the bottom of how messed up I am. But because I am loved, I *can* have the courage to face the reality of my sin. I *can* have the faith to live above the curse of my condition, by the power God gives me moment by moment.

Why Does He Care So Much?

Why does God go to so much trouble for us? Doesn't He have more important things to do? Evidently not. Another one of David's songs goes, *"When I consider Your heavens, the work of Your fingers, the moon and the stars, which You have set in place, what is man that You are mindful of him, the son of man that You care for him?"* (Ps 8:3-4)

The hardest thing in the world for me to believe about God is not that He exists. It is not hard for me to believe that God made the world. It isn't even hard for me to believe that He died on a cross to save a world of sinners. The hardest thing in the world for me to believe about God is that He is madly in love with *me*.

That is the message my heart needs to hear over and over every day. That is the truth that will set me free to live and love and serve and suffer as Jesus wants to do through me. That is what I am learning to trust about Jesus. He loves *me*! That is why I can never be the same. Every day I test the theory that He loves me and it keeps working! No wonder people through the ages have said with David, "Your love, O Lord, is *better* than life!"

So If God Loves Us, What's the Problem?

God won't stop until He gets us back or dies trying. That is what Jesus proved to all who care to look at what He did on the Roman cross. If God cares so much and is passionately pursuing us through the message of Jesus, let's get this show on the road!

But it isn't as easy as we think. The real question is not "Does God want *us*?" The real question is "Do we want *Him*?" God is looking for lovers. Fiery, faithful lovers. He wants to be wanted. He is patiently alluring people around the world, because He does not want any to perish, but all to come to a full realization of who He really is. He wants to marry us! Do we want to get hitched with Him?

He, like any lover, wants His affections returned freely and His desires to be matched. He wants a Bridal People to live with Him forever, who know and love Him for who He is. He will only have a perfect Bride, equally yoked with Him in passion, in purity, and in purpose, forever.

A Passion for Nearness

We have no reference points for who God is or what He is like unless He communicates to us. At Mt. Sinai, Israel was shown as much of God as they could bear. Instead of wanting more, they were terrified. "Sure He is awesome, terrifying, and beautiful, but can we live together?" They must have wondered this. The least amount of revelation God could give them in a corporate setting, was more than they could stand.

Before you are too critical of Israel, realize this; in our day of postmodern, trivializing, Western culture, we have lost the very concept of majestic deity. Our highest concept of God might be a movie or a mountain view. Our generation is about as ready for a five senses encounter with God as a deer standing on railroad tracks blinded by the lights of a runaway freight train.

Lucy and I have three boys. There might have been a couple of times over the thirty years of our marriage that I spoke harshly and frightened them. Okay, more than twice! But an angry father with imperfect emotions is not a good parallel with the Creator of the Universe on his betrothal day with his Bridal People. The people on the plains of Sinai that day were not afraid of God's sternness so much as they were shaken by His *passion for nearness*. He wanted to be closer to them than they wanted Him to be. He wanted intimacy with the whole nation! But for Him to come in His fullness would mean they would all die! That was a real dilemma. (Ex. 19:3-6)

That is *our* dilemma. God wants intimacy with everybody on the planet, but the people living on the planet today are pretty happy with Him not being here. In the relative fact that God is not "visibly" here, we rationalize that He is pretty cool with how things are, too. Not so!

The greatest gift God can ever give to any of us is Himself. He was giving Himself to us in Creation and He continues to give Himself by coming near to us daily in countless, merciful ways. When God comes near to sinful, frail human beings, He has to "hide" himself in some way to protect us from being zapped like a mosquito crashing into a bug light. He speaks tenderly to us first. He suffers long with love, before He shakes us with both tender and severe mercies. He will do whatever it takes, so we will turn to Him and know Him as He really is. He is out to get our attention and He knows how to speak our language, *if* we are listening.

If we do not listen to His offer of Himself through His covenant approaches of love, there is a downside. Are we listening to the language of His love in the details of life and in the pages of Scripture? Is our nation listening? Is the world listening?

The Downside

As with any covenant promise or marriage vow of the time, Yahweh spoke not only about the surpassing sweet things that came with the arrangement, but there was also the part about what happens if you cheat on your Lover. What God laid out for "cheatin' lovers" that day was more graphic than any country music ditty that has ever come out of Nashville. You can read it for yourself, but basically He tells Israel, "If you go after other lovers, I will send you stern warnings. If you do not heed those warnings, I will kill you. But I will not share you with any other being. You are mine. Have a nice day."

It wasn't long before God wanted to kill Israel in the desert, but Moses stopped him with an argument like, "What would the neighbors think?! They won't have a chance to see you show off as you dwell with your Bridal People and love on them as you long to do." What happened in the Desert of Sinai was in some ways a 40 year argument in the bedroom. "Do you love Me or not?"

Ironically, God fashioned the heart of Moses that pleaded with Him for mercy. God delights in mercy, remember. He is slow to anger, abounding in love. Give Him a good reason to "change his mind" and He probably will. He is the author of those passionate prayers you thought you came up with on your own!

He answered Moses' prayer. Over the next forty years Yahweh fashioned a heart of faith in a new generation who would trust His love for them. But all of those who rebelled against Him at Sinai died on the trail to the land of Promise. This is a sobering warning to all future generations. Our God is consuming fire. He is a cosmic hunk of burning love. The destiny of every man and woman is to burn with Him or without Him. But we will burn. The particular kind of angel that cries out "Holy, Holy, Holy" as they circle the fiery throne of God are called cherubim, which means "burning ones."

Some folks like to say the God of the Old Testament is not like the God of the New Testament. Read more closely. The same God who slew His own people in the desert and slew the people of Canaan who lived in the land before Israel, is the same God who will judge every person who has rejected His love for them through Jesus His Son. He is the same God who inspired one of Jesus' best friends, John, to write about terrible judgments to come in the future and especially during the generation before the return of Jesus. This same Jesus who told Peter to put away his sword, will split the heavens and come with a sword to slay the people who thought they were masters of their own universe.

We are on a collision course with the most passionately loving being in the universe. He is not a vengeful, petty God who flies off the handle when He can't have his way. He is a God more patient in his longings, more sacrificial in his workings, more ingenious in his designs, and more dramatic in how He writes the story than we can ever imagine. He is more beautiful than we can grasp, more playful and full of joy than any pleasure in this age, and more gloriously real than what our five senses tell us. No wonder those who choose Him now will be fascinated with Him for all eternity!

A Love Stronger Than Death, Jealousy Unyielding as the Grave

Regardless of the brand of Christianity or other religion you trust most, just know that Jesus talked about what will happen to those who harden their hearts to God. It is a part of His teaching, whether I like it or not, and most of the time I don't. Not because it isn't what He taught or isn't true, but because my understanding of God is so ridiculously tiny compared to His reality. My concept of fairness and His eternal councils are wide apart.

Hell is not a place for the "bad" people, and Heaven is not the place for the "good" people as we may judge those concepts. Hell is not a place that a small god sends really smart people who figured out that he faked the universe after all and we really are the result of randomness, blind matter, and time. Hell is not a place that some people like Hitler and Stalin go to get theirs. Hell is not a place for all the party people to party like it is 1999 while the Devil is the DJ.

Hell is the place that God has prepared for those who have passed by His passionate heart and purpose for them. It is for those who scorn His love. Who scorn Him. He is not hiding. He is giving all with ears to hear opportunities to come to Him.

Beloved, do not forget this one thing, that with the Lord one day is as a thousand years and a thousand years as one day. The Lord is not slack concerning His promise, as some count slackness, but is longsuffering toward us, not willing that any should perish, but that all should come to repentance. (2 Peter 3:8, 9)

When the Holy One of Israel revealed His name to Moses the first time on the mountain out of the burning bush, it was I AM THAT I AM, or Yahweh, the self existent ONE. The second time He revealed His Name on the mountain at the giving of the covenant to the nation, it was, I AM JEALOUS. I *long* to be known and honored by all I have made.

The God who is revealed in scripture and in history is either your greatest friend or your greatest enemy. The Devil is a chump compared to God. God has all the cards and is playing for keeps. He is full of passion and no one can stop Him when He is ready to move.

There is no hiding the "Yes" or "No" in our hearts from this God-Man, Jesus. He is the One appointed as Judge of All. When we stand before Him, all the landscape of our soul is laid bare in His sight. He is our Judge, but He is also our Bridegroom. He wants us to finish well so He can marry us! He is ready to help anyone who asks for His help at any moment! Why? Because *His* greatest desire is to be with *you* forever! Do you *want* to marry Him? Do you even *know* who He is? How *intimately* do you know Him? How we relate *now* to this mysterious Jesus is the secret to finishing His gift of life to us well.

Finishing Life Well

Part Two

Covenant Faithfulness

Chapter 5

Trusting God's Promises

"The LORD is trustworthy in all he promises
and faithful in all he does."
(Psalm 145:13)

Boy Meets Girl

Long before Harry met Sally, long before Homer met Marge, long before Samson met Delilah, the first boy met the first girl. Adam met Eve.

The Bible begins with a wedding and ends with a wedding. Book 1 starts in a Bridal Garden and book 66 ends in a Bridal City.

Gen 2:24: "A man shall leave his father and mother and cleave to his wife and the two shall become one flesh."

Rev. 21:2: "I saw the Holy City, the new Jerusalem, coming down out of heaven from God, prepared as a bride beautifully dressed for her husband."

God marries Adam and Eve in the Garden. God marries Jesus and His Bridal People of all generations in the New Jerusalem. Hmmm... this marriage covenant concept might be pretty serious!

Dirt With Destiny – Bearing the Image of God

Adam means "ground" or "dirt." Eve means "life" or "living". She became the life bearer for us all. In Genesis 5:2, God called them *both* "adam". We are made in God's image, male and female, out of dirt. Dirt with destiny!

Then God said, 'Let us make mankind in our image, in our likeness, so that they may rule over the fish in the sea and the birds in the sky, over the livestock and all the wild animals, and over all the creatures that move along the ground.' So God created mankind in his own image, in the image of God he created them; male and female he created them. (Genesis 1:26-27)

God's plans for intimate partnership with us as His Image Bearers started before time. His desire to govern creation with us included the very blood sacrifice He knew would be necessary before He made us. Jesus is described as the "Lamb of God slain before the foundation of the world." (Revelation 13:8) The cross He would die on one day was not a surprise to the Son of God. Before time and creation, God conceived us in sacrificial love. What a glorious mystery!

God wants His image in the world He made. Bearing the Image of God is the highest privilege of the human race. At creation God made Adam and Eve to bear His image as male and female together. The Garden of Eden was the first meeting place with God. Adam was the first Priest. When Adam disobeyed God, God's image in Adam was marred. His sin brought death. God clothed their nakedness and shame with animal skins.

But God's desire to have a people in the Earth who bear His image and provide a place of encounter is *unrelenting*. In Exodus 19, through Moses, God called Israel to be an Image Bearing *nation*. The priestly tribe of Levi carried God's Tent of Meeting as a sign to the world. "I will make you a light for the Gentiles, that my salvation may reach to the ends of the earth." (Isaiah 49:6)

In Jeremiah 18:6, Israel was clay thrown onto a Potter's wheel and refashioned as an image bearing vessel. Israel, like Adam, failed to faithfully bear God's Image to the world. Through Jeremiah, God says, "'Can I not do with you, Israel, as this potter does?' declares the LORD. 'Like clay in the hand of the potter, so are you in my hand, Israel.'"

God kept calling Israel to her global Image Bearing witness through the prophets up to the time of Jesus. The Temple in Jerusalem was to be a House of Prayer for all Nations. Jesus declared the leaders of Israel had made God's Meeting Place, "A Den of Robbers." When God rejected the Jewish Temple, Jesus became the meeting place of God and men. Jesus is an *eternal* King and High Priest. More than merely bearing God's Image, Jesus is the God-Man.

The Son is the image of the invisible God, the firstborn over all creation. For in him all things were created: things in heaven and on earth, visible and invisible, whether thrones or powers or rulers or authorities; all things have been created through him and for him... For God was pleased to have all his fullness dwell in him, and through him to reconcile to himself all things, whether things on earth or things in heaven, by making peace through his blood, shed on the cross...For in Christ all the fullness of the Deity lives in bodily form. (Colossians 1:15-16, 19-20, 2:9)

When Jesus ascended to Heaven forty days after His resurrection, He sent the Holy Spirit on one hundred and twenty followers gathered in night and day prayer for ten days. (Acts 2) That outpouring of God's Spirit by Jesus birthed the Church for our Age. Now *anyone* can be God's Image Bearer when born of the Holy Spirit. The meeting place of God in the Earth is Jesus in the Human Heart!

Remember that at that time you were separate from Christ, excluded from citizenship in Israel and foreigners to the covenants of the promise, without hope and without God in the world. But now in Christ Jesus you who once were far away have been brought near by the blood of Christ... Consequently, you are no longer foreigners and strangers, but fellow citizens with God's people... In him the whole building is joined together and rises to become a holy temple in the Lord. And in him you too are being built together to become a dwelling in which God lives by his Spirit. (Eph. 2:12-13, 19, 21-22)

God's glory is now placed in ordinary people. "But we have this treasure in jars of clay to show that this all-surpassing power is from God and not from us." (2 Cor. 4:7) Because of our Master Potter, in Christ we go from being just dirt, to dirt with destiny once again!"

Protecting What is Precious

God fashioned marriage as the first human institution. Each marriage between a man and woman is a divine re-enactment of the glorious marriage of Adam and Eve by God in the Bridal Garden. Each marriage is also a divine rehearsal for the Wedding our Father will give Jesus, the Bridegroom King, and His Bride in the Age to come. Marriage is holy to God, because it bears His Image and produces more Image Bearers. Like a secret garden with high walls and secure gates, marriage is to be protected and nurtured; for out of the soil of marriage sprout children!

The pleasures of sexual intimacy are intended within the boundaries of marriage because God wants each man and woman to experience what our first parents knew - the incredible joy of being naked and unashamed in His Presence! The Song of Solomon celebrates this in the Bible. God designed sexuality not merely for having children, but for pure pleasure! Anything we think has great value, we jealously protect. Like precious jewelry in a locked safe, God guards marriages and families. So should we.

Covenant Promises

Everything God makes He sets within boundaries of loyal love sealed with a covenant. A covenant involves a sacred exchange of promises. Covenants carry great blessings when honored and severe consequences when dishonored. The Bible is the storyline of God's gracious covenant promises toward us. It is the account of what happens when we live by God's promises and when we don't. Whether or not we are faithful, God is *always* faithful. A promise is as good as the one making it. The great news is, all of history and creation rests on the character of a Father whose faithful love and has no limits.

"Your kingdom is an everlasting kingdom, and your dominion endures through all generations. The LORD is trustworthy in all he promises and faithful in all he does.

The LORD upholds all who fall and lifts up all who are bowed down. The eyes of all look to you, and you give them their food at the proper time. You open your hand and satisfy the desires of every living thing. The LORD is righteous in all his ways and faithful in all he does. The LORD is near to all who call on him, to all who call on him in truth. He fulfills the desires of those who fear him; he hears their cry and saves them. The LORD watches over all who love him, but all the wicked he will destroy." (Psalm 145:13-20)

Marriage is a covenant with majestic blessings. Being united with someone we love for LIFE? AMAZING! Making new image bearers of God? C'mon, that's WILD! The blessings of marriage fascinate us all, and should. There is an awesome reason we consider risking all for the "happily ever after". But as clay vessels, we also want to know "What happens if...", because we aren't so sure about ourselves or the other party. Commitment takes a leap of faith. Making a unilateral promise to someone for the rest of our life, no matter what happens along the way, is straight up *terrifying*! And should be. We tremble at the thought of binding our flawed self to someone else who isn't perfect. God does it all the time! Because God fights for every covenant, we *can* make them, and with His help, keep them.

God is the greatest lover of all. He binds Himself to our rebellious, "spit in your face" race! He is not afraid of committing Himself to us in spite of our incurable fickleness. He knew what He was getting into when He fashioned us in His own image with a will to obey or disobey. Why did He do that? Why didn't he just make robots? Because as a Lover, God is looking for those who will love Him back. We were *made* for love! God will remove everything that hinders love toward Him. Which, given the fact that we can't seem to keep our own promises, means He will always keep His in order for the relationship to stay alive.

"God is not human, that He should lie, not a human being, that He should change His mind. Does He speak and then not act? Does He promise and not fulfill?" (Nu 23:19)

"He who is the Glory of Israel does not lie or change his mind; for he is not a human being, that he should change his mind." (1 Sam 15:29)

"God did this so that, by two unchangeable things in which it is impossible for God to lie, we who have fled to take hold of the hope set before us may be greatly encouraged." (Heb 6:18)

Trust Issues

I made a mistake with my youngest son, Daniel, one day. We were going to get a shot at the doctor's office. Well, *we* weren't, but he was, and he was very apprehensive about how much pain there might be. The last time I had gone to this same clinic for a shot, it had been virtually painless. I "promised" Daniel that it wouldn't hurt.

It did hurt. How much I really don't know. But it hurt enough that when we got back in the car there was a real trust issue between him and me. After raising two other boys, I had gotten better at measuring truth in my words. But I had blown it with Daniel this time. I should have told him pain was a real possibility, but I was praying with him that it wouldn't be too bad.

God never fails to keep a promise. Even if it doesn't happen for a long time, *or even in our lifetime*, He *will* keep His promises. His promises extend not only to us, but to our children if they stay true to the same promises. We have a difficult time thinking multi-generationally. We see ourselves as the whole story. But true significance is being swept up in a story so vast it can only be told in eternity. Guess what? That is what happens when we marry GOD! We live forever and become a part of His Story.

If we are to become promise keepers who finish life well, we need an *eternal perspective*. God is taking care of the universe without our help and His plans for history can't be changed. When we make our life the reference point for whether or not God is in control, we get mad and walk away. In the traditional Black church there is a familiar saying, "God is good all the time." Knowing that truth is better than anything we could learn in a seminary.

God is a Just Judge

The God of the Bible takes no pleasure in pointless suffering. He, more than anyone, knows how broken our world is. He could have ended history the day Adam sinned. Adam's disobedience brought chaos, futility, cruelty, and death. The age old accusation of the atheist and agnostic shouts, "If there is a god and he is good, why is there pain and suffering in the world?" Pain raises accusations in our hearts toward God. "Don't you care?!" "Why is this happening to me?" We all think this at different times.

The biblical view of history is that all suffering in this broken world has meaning because God is more than *just* a Bridegroom King. God is a Perfect Judge and there *will* be a Day of Judgment. If that is not true, our lives *are* meaningless and there *is* no justice. But all who bear *or* cause injustice have God as their advocate when they cry to Him. Oppressors need God more than their victims. They just don't realize it as easily.

God came in the man Jesus to enter the full spectrum of our human experience. Jesus identified with the oppressed, but He forgave His oppressors. Jesus' suffering and death demonstrates how God has taken all our pain and suffering seriously by bearing it Himself. Because Jesus conquered sin and death as a Man and now sits on the Throne of Heaven as God, He *can* rightfully avenge every injustice and wipe away every tear in history. We *can* open our hearts to Him in our pain, knowing that He has fought for us on the cross. Jesus will return to right every wrong and turn our mourning into dancing at the end of the Age.

God's answer to the question, "Do you care?!" is answered with a "Yes!" written with covenant love in His own blood.

Promises Sealed in Blood

Blood is part of every covenant in the Bible. Sometimes you have to look between the lines as when Jonathan, the son of Israel's King Saul, made a covenant of friendship with David. David, who in all respects should have been Jonathan's rival to the throne, was the one Jonathan regarded as better than himself. They both vowed to die to remain loyal to the friendship.

During the "old covenant" Passover Meal, Jesus called His bodily sacrifice on the cross a "new covenant" in His blood, poured out to cleanse the sins of any who would receive Him. He died for our friendship and for the marriage!

At the first wedding God performs a "rib-ectomy" on Adam under anesthesia. He puts Adam to sleep and opens his flesh. Blood is implied here. God takes out a rib bone and uses the DNA to make Eve. God saved His best work for last! Adam exclaimed, "Bone of my bone! Flesh of my flesh!" when he saw his "Whoa – Man!". The consummation of a marriage in physical union is usually accompanied by the blood of the virgin woman. By implication, the blood of both Adam and Eve were a part of the first marriage.

Abraham is the father of faith in God because he believed God's promises to him. God made a covenant with him in Genesis 15. In the ancient world, covenant terms were announced and sealed with oaths which included a "maledictory curse". Each party swore death on themselves if they broke the covenant. The blood of animals called creation as a witness. "If I break this covenant, may my blood be shed as it has been done with these animals."

In Genesis 15, the covenant between Abram and God takes place in the midst of a bloody mess. Three of five creatures: a cow, a goat, a ram, a dove and a pigeon are carved in half and placed on the ground. The stage is now set for Abram and God (represented by a smoking pot of fire), to pass between the pieces of torn flesh in a figure 8 motion, each starting from opposite ends of the gauntlet.

Something unusual happens. Like God did to Adam during the rib surgery, He put Abram into a trance-like state. Then *God takes Abram's end of the covenant as well as His own!* God is saying "If I break the covenant, let it be done to me as it is done to these animals, and, if *you* break the covenant let it be done to ME as it is done to these animals."

This is a foreshadowing of God, through Jesus, taking on the curse of all covenant breakers by dying on the cross. Jesus not only initiated the New Covenant, He sealed it with His blood. Jesus bore the curse of all Adam's race and became a bloody mess for the sake of keeping a promise of love. God announced through the prophet Isaiah, hundreds of years before Jesus came, that one day there would be a Servant who would bear the sins of the world.

He was despised and rejected by mankind, a man of suffering, and familiar with pain. Like one from whom people hide their faces he was despised, and we held him in low esteem. Surely he took up our pain and bore our suffering, yet we considered him punished by God, stricken by him, and afflicted. But he was pierced for our transgressions, he was crushed for our iniquities; the punishment that brought us peace was on him, and by his wounds we are healed. (Isaiah 53:3-5)

On the cross, Jesus bore our image as a dirty, cursed people. Anyone can look at Jesus there and be healed from all that is not right. Only the blood of Jesus can save a soul on this planet. It does not matter if it is a Hindu soul, Muslim soul, homosexual soul, or fine church-going soul. "There is *no other name* under Heaven, given among men, by which we MUST be saved." (Acts 4:12) Jesus bore every sin *and* covered it with His noble blood. Jesus kept God's promise of covenant love. He is the most glorious image of Man *and* the most glorious image of God in one moment on the cross. He is the *only* One worthy of all worship. Allelujah!

Chapter 6

Sexual Holiness

"But among you there must not be even a hint of sexual immorality, or of any kind of impurity, or of greed, because these are improper for God's holy people." Eph. 5:3

Before Cold Mountain

Years ago a novel stayed on the best seller lists and minds of many American readers; Charles Frazier's *Cold Mountain*. It was a story of war, romance, friendship, a society in upheaval, an odyssey into the human soul, and two people who just wanted to be left alone to build a simple life. You know, normal novel stuff.

Why is it so hard for people who have found true love to finally enjoy each other? No sooner does Jude Law's character in the movie version meet Nicole Kidman's character and whoosh, he is off to fight a tragic war far from home. Disillusioned by the carnage and deprivation of the Civil War, his one passion is to get back to the woman he loves. But will she still love him?

Cold Mountain is a real place. It is almost visible from where I am writing this chapter in the mountains of North Carolina. As a young man, I camped in the Shining Rock Wilderness Area next to Cold Mountain. My first son was baptized in the freezing waters of the Pigeon River beneath Cold Mountain. And in Haywood County, where Inman met Ada in the novel, I met the woman of my dreams, Lucy Downey.

I was a Methodist preacher's kid working construction at the church conference grounds at Lake Junaluska in the summer of 1978. I didn't know Jesus, drank beer, chewed tobacco, had lost my license twice drag racing my '67 GTO on city streets, and shamelessly watched every pretty girl who walked by the site. I had a pretty good redneck resume! But, I was also going to college. I was a part of the United Methodist Church for which the hotel we were building would be used. And I was the only one with the courage to go meet the pretty girl who walked past our site on her way to work at the church office next door.

For those who have seen the movie Cold Mountain, the scene where Inman first lays eyes on Ada, is virtually the same as when I first saw Lucy. Inman was working construction with a team building a church for a little Haywood County town. Ada rides by in a buggy next to her preacher Dad. Bam! Love at first sight! Did I mention Lucy's Dad is a Preacher? Creepy huh?

I have a weird movies-mirroring-life gig going on. But there, the similarity ends. Lucy and I have a life far more romantic and adventuresome than Jude Law and Nicole Kidman's characters! We have traveled the world following the leadership of Jesus. Lucy was nearly killed by cross-fire during a Russian Mafia hit in Latvia. During a mission I led to Tajikistan, I was air ambulanced in the middle of the night out of Central Asia to Istanbul, Turkey. We have had a blast raising three amazing sons while helping to lead city-wide and state-wide prayer movements. Dare I say, we are on a mission to transform our whole generation in the grace of God from our home in Birmingham? Hollywood is infatuated with the drama of the romantic chase. Once you get the girl, they start rolling the credits. Not so in real life. I got to marry my girl, *then* the fun really started!

Don't get me wrong. The chase is awesome! When I fell in love with Lucy, there were three years of poems, hand-picked wild flower bouquets, ridiculously long phone conversations, and syrupy love letters (before Facebook there was this thing called the US Postal service). But if you were to ask me to trade those three years of dating with any three years of our marriage, I would take any three years of our marriage...hands down.

The Vanishing Age of Innocence

Marriage is great, but it doesn't cure a sinful nature. Only God does that. "Bent-ness" is our nature and our choices. Pick your brand of sexual bent-ness. Mine was heterosexual promiscuity for two years in college before meeting Lucy and Jesus. My introduction to naked women began as a kid. My neighborhood buddies and I would get on our bikes and go junk pile raiding. We weren't looking for pornography. We were interested in finding anything cool. I once found a whole bag full of Austrian coins. Every now and then we would find a pinup magazine and take it to our fort. A kid these days doesn't have to dig through trash piles to find pornography. Mom and dad have saved him calories by piping it right through the flat screen HDTV. If the regular cable menu isn't easy enough to get to porn, then a couple of clicks on the internet will take you to anything you want to see.

We live in an R rated society on its way to XXX. According to the 2011 e-book, "Parenting the Internet Generation" on covenanteyes. com, 93% of boys and 62% of girls have been exposed to internet pornography before age 18. These stats, sadly, sound low to me. One of the most important things a head of household can do is make their property and internet devices porn-free. Getting filtering technology, like Covenant Eyes, is absolutely necessary to keeping pace with new technology. Exposure to hard core pornography of every kind is accessible to more people at a younger age through more devices, i.e. cell phones, e-book readers, and iPods. As of the printing of this chapter, Covenant Eyes, like many companies attempting to keep the toxic waste of "pornolution" out of our hearts, has no filtering technology for mobile internet devices like iPhones, iPod touches, and iPads. Mobicip.com does.

I was recently given an e-book reader and discovered there was NO parental control on the device other than to disable the internet. When I called their customer service to ask why Mobicip.com would not download to my device, I was told it would not work. When I asked what would filter out pornography, I was informed there was no filtering product currently compatible with their product. I was put on a list of others who had inquired, but no timetable was offered for when it would be safe from pornography! This was happening while commercials for this product were airing kids and parents cuddling in bed reading together. Is anyone awake? That same children's e-book reader is an unfiltered pornographic gateway.

My question is, "Why is it that pornographers have the cultural upper hand when it comes to internet and cable gate-keeping protocols?" Whenever I have signed up for cable, I have to OPT OUT of getting the highly damaging imagery on those channels. It wouldn't violate free speech laws to have pornography channels available as an OPT IN. But as a parent, the burden is on me to going through a period of time (even if it is only ten minutes) where someone from the cable or satellite company walks me through the steps to lock the toxic channels.

Why are the laws such that they favor the pornographers polluting the next generation and not the parents protecting the next generation?

Why are Apple, Microsoft, and other software companies, with all their resources and technological brilliance, designing internet ready devices in the hands of millions of youth and children with browsers that offer NO automatic protection from pornography? This is cultural insanity! Why is no one in the product design phase asking "Since pornography is spiritually devastating for children and children use our devices, why don't we design browsers so the adults who want pornography have to buy a separate browser or go through an OPT IN protocol?" The answer is painfully obvious. Billions of dollars are on the side of those profiting from the marketing of sexual imagery.

The result is a world where women continue to be victimized and exploited, young children continue to be exposed to things they should never see even as an adult, a global sex industry with child trafficking is fueled, marriages and families continue to be undermined, and pedophiles continue to have an easy avenue for recruitment.

No More Millstones!

A radical, but simple, solution would be for the Federal Communications Commission (FCC) to protect our children from toxic "pornolution" by mandating a G or PG-rated default for the internet, with opt-ins for R, and XXX. This would NOT violate free speech. It would simply move the line of internet protocols and require devices that are internet ready to begin with a G-rated default.

Every on-line device today is a pornographic event in the hands of our children waiting to happen. An age of innocence for the moral development of the next generation is worth fighting for. Our government needs to make the pornographers and pedophiles trudge through the thicket of inconvenient and costly protocols that parents now hack through. We need corporate and government leaders who believe sexuality is a gift to be cherished and protected, not a commodity to be bought and sold.

"Jesus said to his disciples: 'Things that cause people to stumble are bound to come, but woe to anyone through whom they come. It would be better for them to be thrown into the sea with a mill-stone tied around their neck than to cause one of these little ones to stumble. So watch yourselves.'" (Luke 17:1-3)

The zeal of God is against those who cause damage to children. The image of a huge stone necklace sinking someone like an anchor is better than the judgment God feels is appropriate for a pornographer marketing to children, child molesters, pedophiles, and the like. We as a country are in grave danger of great judgment from God precisely because corporate and government America is selling our children to sex-filled media for the sake of moving billions of dollars in products and services.

Paul McHugh, University Distinguished Service Professor of Psychiatry at Johns Hopkins University School of Medicine, is one of several leading professors and social scientists who spoke at "The Social Cost of Pornography," an interdisciplinary consultation at Princeton University in 2009. He warned, "Multimedia pornography has become the chief means by which the emergent sex industry encourages the solicitations of the senses to overwhelm the moral and aesthetic feelings of fitness on which all civilized actions and an ordered culture depend. Pornography represents the contemporary means of making Caligulas of us all—with all that that implies in terms of violence, misogyny, and interpersonal grief."

Caligula was a Roman Emperor who was infamous for his lack of moral boundaries.

The report of Dr. McHugh and others can be found on The Witherspoon Institute web-site (winst.org). There you can view free videos or order "The Social Cost of Pornography", the compendium of presentations exposing the high risks of mainstreaming pornography into our society.

Another fine educational resource is Morality in Media and their web-site, Pornharms.com. Pat Trueman, the former lead Justice Department prosecutor for obscene pornography cases, directs this site which keeps the public informed with up-to-date reports, research, and efforts to restrict obscene and child pornography which, though illegal under Federal law, is no longer enforced.

Public opinion and political will takes time to develop. But with the painful relational and social costs of pornography becoming more obvious to all, reasonable measures for filtering hard core, violent, and child pornography could regain popular appeal. Until the cultural battles are won, we must fight the battles in our own hearts and in our homes.

Time to Take Out the Dirty Laundry

For over twenty-five years I served a college campus ministry that hosted huge global mission conventions. Over 20,000 people, mostly collegians, from all over North America would gather every three years. During the 1990 "Urbana" Mission Convention a woman on the platform prayed, "It is time to take out the dirty laundry!" I was pierced with grief in that moment over my utter sexual brokenness.

For nine years of our marriage, I had been trying to overcome my compulsion to masturbate or view pornography. Lucy was the kind of wife that wanted me to tell her my failures. Every time I fell hurt us both deeply. There is no way to convince a wife that her husband's "bad habit" has nothing to do with her worth and attractiveness. One might wonder if I was fit for ministry at all. Was I a ticking time bomb waiting to go off? Talk about a mixture of fears and desires. That was me and Lucy.

At Urbana conventions most attendees were housed in the dorms of the University of Illinois. Staff, like me, came days early to prepare. It wasn't long before I found pornography in a desk drawer left by the students on break. I fell in to the same old sin even as I heard voices of ministry colleagues in the hall.

Admit, Submit, Commit

Under the weight of the Holy Spirit, I *admitted* to myself and a friend the next day that I was addicted to pornography. I had never let the word "addict" cross my lips before. Through that honesty God began a work I can only describe as miraculous. A pattern of sin ingrained since I was twelve years old was overpowered by the Spirit of God. For the first time in over twenty years, I was free of that compulsion. I *submitted* the storyline of my healing to Lucy and trusted others for accountability.

I didn't want my sons to have the same depth of struggle in that area as their father. A month later I knelt at the foot of my bed after a Sunday afternoon nap. My two young sons were still asleep in front of me. I felt the presence of God as I *committed* my mind and imagination back to Him. I also covenanted, by His grace, never to offer my hands or body in any unclean act again. My sons were on what had now become an altar. The marriage bed *is* an altar that God does not want to be defiled. I knew I wasn't just making a covenant with God for myself. My actions as a father, directly or indirectly, would affect generations to come.

The undefeated sin patterns of one generation influence the next, until a "new covenant" in the blood of Jesus is made. On this issue at least, God had overcome a generational pattern of addiction. My sons have their own journey ahead of them. I am trying not to be silent or absent where sexual purity in their lives is concerned. Talking about sex honestly isn't easy, but disengagement from conversation about sexuality results in disaster for our kids. If you are looking for help, I recommend PamStenzel.com. Pam's compelling message is geared for teens, but is relevant for anyone wanting to know the truth about sex outside marriage and its consequences.

Walking in the Light of God's Spirit

Biblical maturity is not measured as moral perfection. It is measured by the speed and depth of repentance. It is humility. It is how quickly we admit our sin, submit to truth in community, and commit ourselves to holiness. God's mercy is not given for delaying repentance. Why endure years of agony, when by God's mercy, we can face the pain of our sinful actions in minutes? *His mercy is given for enjoying His Presence, not for enjoying our sin.*

"God is light; in him there is no darkness at all. If we claim to have fellowship with him and yet walk in the darkness, we lie and do not live out the truth. But if we walk in the light, as he is in the light, we have fellowship with one another, and the blood of Jesus, his Son, purifies us from all sin. If we claim to be without sin, we deceive ourselves and the truth is not in us. If we confess our sins, he is faithful and just and will forgive us our sins and purify us from all unrighteousness. If we claim we have not sinned, we make him out to be a liar and his word is not in us." (1 John 1:5-10)

Walking in the light is a lifestyle of truthfulness. God's Spirit of Truth shines into the dark corners of our hearts. A constant prayer life is essential to growing in God. Prioritize personal prayer in your daily schedule. Be a part of a praying church. Find a prayer partner at school or on the job. Find a night and day praying community near you or on the web-stream.

A deep prayer life helps us turn from vain thoughts before they hatch into deeds. "You have heard that it was said, 'You shall not commit adultery. But I tell you that anyone who looks at a woman lustfully has already committed adultery with her in his heart.'" (Matt 5:27-28)

If there are deeds, the Holy Spirit empowers us to change before there are more deeds. If admitting failures to God privately isn't breaking the pattern, admit your failures to a trusted follower of Jesus and let them pray for God's Spirit to wash and fill you. "Confess your sins to one another and pray for one another, that you may be healed." (James 5:16.)

Walking in the light of the Holy Spirit is the normal Christian life. Holiness is not a track record, it is the track! Holiness is the God-ward direction of our heart. We become holy not by focusing on ourselves and our performance, but on God and His performance. Don't buy the lie that sexual purity is impossible in our culture today. Sexual holiness is *inevitable*, as we walk with the Holy One!

Chapter 7

The Tumbler of Community

*"God is faithful; he will not let you be tempted beyond
what you can bear. But when you are tempted, he will also
provide a way out so that you can stand up under it."*
(1 Cor 10:13)

You Are Not Alone

After 1990 I served on prayer ministry teams at five more
Urbana Student Mission Conventions. We taught on God's
power to heal and forgive and prayed with students who wanted help.
Thousands of students attended these sessions. I cannot describe
the devastating stories I heard as we went to Jesus in prayer. There
were things that young people were experiencing that I could not
have imagined. I mean that. I heard things that I really didn't think
could ever happen to anyone on God's green earth. But they did.
I became aware that sexual addictions were no longer mainly guy
issues. Women addicted to pornography, masturbation, promiscuity,
and same sex attraction were quickly closing the gap.

Not all were from confessing Christian homes, but these were
Christian kids. Not only that, they were collegians, the elite of our
society. And all were sexually bent, among many other ways of
being bent. We gathered the male students to deal with our sexual
lives. The auditorium was filled by the hundreds. The lines for prayer

went until we were chased out by security. I understood then that the sexual tsunami was already crashing onto our cultural shores.

The good news is, the Holy Spirit *never* gets tired of cleaning up people who ask. No matter how many times we fall down, if we want to be picked up, He *will* pick us up. This is a therapist's nightmare. But not for God! Why did Jesus go to the cross? He went to obliterate our impenetrable sin problem because it was keeping us from enjoying Him and Him enjoying us! God will remove anything that hinders intimacy with Him, if we let Him.

It is the job of the Holy Spirit to clean us up and He is good at it. He enjoys it. Let's keep coming to Him. Let's pray quickly and often. Jesus knows about the other 99 issues in our hearts we aren't in touch with yet and He still loves us! No matter how many times we fall in the mud let's jump in Daddy's arms and not worry about staining His shirt.

But here is the question... Do we really *want* to be healed so that we can be with Him? Let's be honest on that one.

Getting clean and going right back into the mud won't do us any good. No matter what the sin, we are going to have to change from the inside out with radical honesty every step of the way. It will mean staying close to Jesus, and His community of friends, the rest of our lives. It will mean a *lifestyle* of repentance and prayer.

Running the Race in Covenant Community

The community of Jesus is a covenant community. That means we are "stuck" with each other. We rub against each other's rough edges like semi-precious stones thrown into a tumbler. Remember the tumbler? I had one in high school. You put rough gem stones into a rolling container driven by a little motor. Then you add sand for friction and water for smoothing. Flip the switch and listen to an annoying grinding sound for a month and voila! A beautiful smooth stone is the product of time and friction.

The friction of conflict over time in authentic grace-filled community is how God polishes us into His beautiful likeness. Remaining true to imperfect, but gracious communities of Jesus strugglers, is how we get healed and shaped into a people who look like Jesus.

The pursuit of God was never meant to be a solo journey. We run after Jesus in the company of flawed friends. "Let *us* run with perseverance the race marked out for *us*, looking to Jesus the pioneer and polisher of *our* faith." (Hebrews 12:1-2)

There are no quick fixes! All of human history is one big Tumbler. The great news of the Bible is that God chose to put *Himself* in *our* Tumbler! For thirty-three years Mary and Joseph's kid rubbed up against us. We hated Him for the depth of His honesty about God, Himself, ourselves, and the whole mess of screwed up dead religion and corrupt government. While we spat on Him, whipped Him, cursed Him, and killed Him, He just kept right on tumbling. He tumbled into our grave and He tumbled right out again in three days. It was the best day ever!

If you are not in a Jesus worshipping community of some kind, find one. Take your time. No community is perfect. Some are more pain than they are worth. But don't think you can grow into a robust follower of Jesus on your own. We were made for love and truth expressed in Christ centered relationships. We are all doing God together. It is fine to move from one community to another as long as you always remember you can never get out of the tumbler of life. Some communities we choose and others are chosen for us. But all of us are products of human interaction, for better or for worse. Thank God He sent Jesus to live in our tumbler and begin the thousands of years of polishing that will lead us into a Forever Family of Affection.

Jesus said, "It is the sick, who know they have need of a doctor, who will receive healing." Jesus came for those who were not deluded about their own condition. Don't use the fact of your brokenness or anyone else's as an excuse not to go to Jesus yourself. Life is too short and you are too valuable. But if you choose to avoid Jesus, be careful you do not hinder others on their way to him. That will *really* tick God off.

Worth the Fight

Long lines of people needing help can be overwhelming. A few minutes of prayer feels like putting a band-aid on a grenade wound.

But long lines of broken people turning to Jesus give me hope. Those who are eventually rescued from patterns of sin, and the downward spiral of introspection that go with them, make me want to shout!

I have no condemnation toward anyone in sexual brokenness. There are no "rocks in my pockets." I have comforted young men *and* young women sobbing over their pornographic, promiscuous, and homosexual desires and their lack of hope they will ever change. I have close friends who have slipped into the prevailing sexual confusion of our culture. We are in a spiritual conflict with real casualties. But I have *many* more friends with the same desires for whom the love of Jesus has restored their sexual holiness.

Jesus cannot be manipulated. He is not fooled by our religious games, social propaganda, and philosophic rationalizations. If we want to get past the junk to the good part, it means growing a life of honest prayer. If we don't want to be healed, we need to tell him that. If the best we can say is, "Jesus, I *want to want* to be healed," He can work with that. He can put desires in us that we don't have. How cool is that?

We may not always want something good for ourselves. But do we want something good for our kids? Our wife or husband? Our girlfriend or boyfriend? Our Mom or Dad? Is there a healthy fear of the Lord? Jesus said, "If your right eye causes you to sin, pluck it out! Better to enter Heaven with one eye, than to enter Hell with two." (Matthew 5:29) That is intense. But knowing that the God who brought us in to this world can also take us out has saved more than one poor fool from disaster.

If you have left the community of those who are on the journey to wholeness in Christ, maybe this is your invitation to return. The tsunamis of the fallen world buffet us all. We are all tumbling in their crashing waves. Let's all tumble forward together with Jesus.

Chapter 8

Marriage on Trial

*"Anyone who listens to the word but does not do what it says is
like a man who looks at his face in a mirror and, after looking at
himself, goes away and immediately forgets what he looks like."*
(James 1:23-24)

The Politics of Sexuality

America has lost her moral compass. The federal government cannot fix our sexual rampage and marriage delusion. Problems with spiritual roots aren't solved by laws. Laws are reflections of spiritual realities, of *us*. Too many lawmakers, and the people who vote for them, have their own issues that rob them of the clear moral judgment any good dad would have for his kids. Many laws impose low moral standards rather than protect high ones.

Unjust and immoral businesses are multi-billion dollar industries. It is difficult for people committed to justice and righteousness to fight the long expensive legal battles to change the myriad of laws protecting destructive social practices. Even then, changing laws won't necessarily change behavior. Only spiritual awakening anchored to the heart of Jesus will change our generation.

We live during a period in America when the rules of sexual engagement are being rewritten at a rollercoaster rate. We believe sexual desires are beyond our self-control. There is plenty of anecdotal evidence to support that idea. We *are* out of control!

Our belief in an individual's freedom to pursue happiness has birthed a movement of "sexual entitlement rights." The "right to privacy" was invented by our Supreme Court to justify the *Roe vs. Wade* ruling of 1973 that made killing babies in Eve's womb legal in America. This codified the sovereignty of an individual to assert their right to happiness through sexual and economic freedom over people not yet born. The "right" to privacy is a legal fig leaf used to cover our collective shame and social cowardice.

Taking a human life should never be a "right" and should not be "private." A woman has a right to make decisions concerning her own body, but the baby in her womb *is not her body*. There is another image bearer growing inside that the Master Potter is fashioning.

Combine our belief in the sovereignty of personal happiness with our lack of understanding for God and His design for men and women and you have the ripe conditions for our cultural acceleration toward no meaningful legal boundaries at all. In the midst of so much confusion, the media campaign of those addicted to a same sex attraction has taken significant root in our social mindset.

The Flaw of Making Preferences a Civil Right

Many social movements link their cause to the high moral ground of the Civil Rights movement of the 1950's and '60's. It has been an effective tactic toward gaining special rights for a persecuted minority, whether it is the unborn, or the homosexual community.

Linking homosexual rights to the Civil Rights movement is, however, fundamentally flawed. Skin tone is genetic. Sexual preference is not. It is, as stated, a preference, a desire. Being a person in the womb is genetic. Being lesbian is not.

Sexual desires may *feel* impossible for us to overcome. It would be easy to think we were created with those desires. We all have desires that cross moral boundaries. But no desire is genetic or beyond God's help for a willing clay vessel to govern, in spite of what we prefer to believe. With all the media hoopla and extensive mapping of the human genome, there has never been indisputable evidence of a homosexual gene. Desires are not genetic. Desires are mental and spiritual.

Let me illustrate what I mean. Kleptomania is the term for people who have an overwhelming desire to steal things for odd psychological reasons. It is not a genetic phenomenon. Kleptomania is a psychological phenomenon with spiritual roots. As far as we know, there is not a gene that makes people want to steal things, but some people struggle with this urge in an unusual way.

If I was a kleptomaniac, I would love for scientists to find a gene that gets me off the social hook. If I have no choice but to steal, how can I be held accountable for stealing? "God" made me with overpowering desires to steal, so he must condone this behavior of mine. Then I would rally the kleptomaniac community to initiate a political process and media campaign with really articulate kleptomaniacs to convince the non-stealing community it is necessary for people born with this desire to steal without any shame or threat of punishment.

Some may think I am wrong about the absence of a genetic basis for behavioral preferences. But while you are searching for non-politicized studies, remember: we are filled with desires because God is full of desires and we are made in His image. Because we are bent, our desires delude us in all kinds of ways. We need God to straighten us out. We must ask Him to place His passions in us.

I am not saying that desires aren't real. They are. I am not saying desires aren't able to overpower people. They do. I am not saying that people whose desires include same sex attraction are not lovable, creative, God-image bearing people. They are. I am saying there is not a proven genetic link and it is likely to never be so. Why?

Because we would likely not survive as a human race if we were all homosexual. A homosexual gene could only be passed through heterosexual activity. Homosexuals are dependent on adoptions or sperm donors to have families.

Rationalizing Sin

What if we start trying to find a gene for *every* human behavior? If we found a gene for pyromania would we create special laws that protect people who love to start fires? Could we protect the ones who struggle with their pyromania, but hold accountable those who commit arson? If we found a gene for self righteousness, could we protect the ones who struggle with judging others, but hold accountable those who verbalize their prejudices? Laws shouldn't dictate consequences for thoughts, but laws should dictate consequences for actions.

While DNA studies may not resolve the human behavior riddle, other body chemistry issues do factor in. Scientists see certain brain activity associated with particular behaviors. Sometimes there is a chemical dependency and sometimes there is a psychological dependency. I have a coffee habit that is both chemical and psychological. I really like cheeseburgers though I know raw broccoli is better for me. A recent study claimed to show differences in brain activity between political conservatives and liberals. Since we probably can't blame our behavior on our DNA hardwiring, perhaps chemical soft wiring will justify our compelling behaviors and beliefs.

I believe brain studies do prove life experiences make powerful chemical impressions that set our thoughts, emotions, and wills on a particular path. Repeated activity causes well worn "grooves" in our synapses. But brain chemistry *can be changed*, whereas, genetics cannot. New pathways from new experiences can be blazed. Surgery and hormone therapy can cosmetically alter a person's gender, but even for a transgender person, sexual preferences are determined primarily by psychology, not chemistry. Brain chemistry is *descriptive* of human behavior, not *prescriptive*.

Sexual preference is heavily influenced by powerful early sexual encounters that produce chemical patterns. Experiences causing brain pathways can be physical or visual. The contact can be voluntary, through coercion, or by neglect. A well meaning parent who unwittingly exposes their child to XXX rated behavior through an unfiltered internet device lives with the tragic loss of innocence that results. Causal experiences can be imprinted at precognitive ages. Compassion for people damaged by those events is required of us all. But the question before our society is, should the cravings springing from any or every sexual neurosis be legally accommodated such that *every* child is at risk?

The trend in America is that homosexual desires should be legally accommodated and mainstreamed into public school curriculum. Then where do you draw the line? What if I am sexually attracted to children, as many in our world now are through child pornography? What makes a pedophile different from a desperate housewife? Should we teach school children that cheating on your spouse is normative simply because so many people desire to do it?

Abandoning traditional marriage as a government standard is social suicide. America may think its biggest enemy is global terrorism or the struggling global economy, but America's biggest enemy is spiritual decay. No society can survive the disintegration of the marriage and family. Political leaders of both major parties seem willing to stare down the barrel of cultural self-destruction for the sake of winning voting blocks. How did we get here?

I Have Seen the Enemy and He is US

It has been a long slow road, but I do not blame our secular culture. I blame the lack of a clear moral voice and example from the Church. Those who claim to know God are in confusion, division, and delusion.

The institutional Church has fumbled many balls, including the marriage ball. Whole denominations of respectable Reformation churches have sold out traditional marriage as the biblical standard. Evangelical leaders preach sexual holiness and practice the very deeds they claim to hate in secret. Horrible sexual abuse scandals by priests have undermined the witness of Roman Catholicism worldwide. God uses secular media to rightly trumpet moral compromise in the Church. The institutional Church; like national Israel, and like Adam and Eve, has failed to clearly bear the Image of God to the world. But God is not done with us yet.

Many hear "God so loved the world" and think God is okay with anything goes. On the contrary, the "anything goes" mentality is what God loves us enough to rescue us from. *"For God so loved the world that he gave his one and only Son, that whoever believes in him shall not perish but have eternal life. For God did not send his Son into the world to condemn the world, but to save the world through him.*

Whoever believes in him is not condemned, but whoever does not believe stands condemned already because they have not believed in the name of God's one and only Son." (John 3:16-18)

Denial

"This is the verdict: Light has come into the world, but people loved darkness instead of light because their deeds were evil. Everyone who does evil hates the light, and will not come into the light for fear that their deeds will be exposed. But whoever lives by the truth comes into the light, so that it may be seen plainly that what they have done has been done in the sight of God." (John 3:19-21)

We LOVE our deeds of darkness and HATE anyone who exposes them. Even without a messenger to shoot, we have a love/hate relationship with our sin. We love the passing pleasure of our sin, but we hate the inescapable shame and guilt that comes with it. If there were no voices saying sexual activity outside of covenant marriage were wrong, people practicing those behaviors would still experience debilitating shame and guilt over time. Judgment for immorality is built into our "spiritual DNA" through our conscience. Self-hatred cannot be blamed on God or His perfect desires for us. He gets to set the terms.

The same process of denial when Adam and Eve disobeyed God happens when we are ashamed of our brokenness. First we run and hide. Then, if we come out of hiding, we team up with other similarly broken people to redefine the world around us in terms that normalize our brokenness. We want to feel good about ourselves, so we clay people start to tell the Potter where *He* got it wrong. We are amazingly bold and creative in our delusion.

Just ask the white people in my part of the country what we did for decades on the issue of race. We had whole churches that rationalized our collective sin of racism toward non-Whites or non-Protestants. We got angry at anyone who challenged our lifestyle or version of Christianity. We changed the very concept of the gospel so that we did not have to deal with our systemic race issue. We went further and used the Bible to justify our hateful or indifferent behavior as God's will. It was pathetic but too few saw it that way at the time. What will future generations think of us concerning our moral delusion concerning sexuality?

Because of the erosion of biblical morality, our secular culture labels any attempt to protect traditional marriage as bigotry, potentially punishable by law. God help us all if we reach the tipping point of delusion where sexual purity is called evil and sexual perversion becomes the institutional social standard.

Sin No More

God does not want to define us by our sin; He wants to define us by His Son. What a difference one letter in the English alphabet can make. I do not believe anyone is "gay". That is buying a line of thinking God does not want anyone to accept. To label ourselves by a particular bent activity plays to the hand of our powerful Enemy who wants to control us *with* that false identity. The deepest truth about anyone's identity is we are loved by God more than our sin can ever undo. Love wins. But love doesn't leave us in our miserable pit.

Remember the woman caught in the act of adultery who was brought by her accusers to Jesus? Instead of joining those who wanted to stone her according to the Law of Moses, He disarmed the mob by saying, "Let him who is without sin cast the first stone." Don't you just love Jesus for saying that?! Then, privately, He asks her, "Woman, where are your accusers?" "Nowhere, Sir." "Then neither do I condemn you. Go and do not sin anymore." (John 8:1-11)

When the guys with rocks in their pockets left, Jesus did not give the woman a "nudge, nudge, wink, wink." God delights to show mercy, but it is not "unsanctified mercy." God doesn't excuse sin. He wants recognition of our sin and its consequences to drive us to His mercy so we share His passion for purity. Jesus said. "Those who have been forgiven much, love much." Loving Jesus with our sexuality means honoring marriage as God's standard.

Reclaiming the Honor of Marriage

Marriage as male and female in joyful companionship and child-bearing union is beyond intelligent debate as the biblical standard. Sexual union is a covenant relationship that models the mystery of Jesus Christ and His Bridal people.

"Submit to one another out of reverence for Christ. Wives, submit to your husbands, as to the Lord. For the husband is the head of the wife as Christ is the head of the Church, His body, of which He is Savior.

Husbands, love your wives, just as Christ loved the church and gave Himself up for her to make her holy... and to present her to Himself as a radiant church... In the same way, husbands ought to love their wives as their own bodies...This is a profound mystery – but I am talking about Christ and the church." (Eph. 5:21-23)

Marriage in scripture is an exclusively *heterosexual* concept. Secular lawmakers can make civil unions and gay marriages with the stroke of a pen. But marriage as one man and one woman in life-long faithfulness is legislated from Heaven. God has his fingerprints all over that one and He is not changing His mind for our sake.

God has given us a unique role to bear His image. We are the only creatures who can choose to love and worship God. We are the only creatures He has died to redeem. We did not descend from apes, we descended from God.

Jesus models what we are to look like as a redeemed humanity. We are to reflect His character and match His desires. Jesus was sexually pure as an unmarried man. But His Wedding Day is set and His Global Bride is preparing herself in passion and purity around the world throughout the generations. The Holy Spirit is giving us beauty treatments and cleaning us up for that consummation. Jesus describes what finishing well looks like in the last verses of the Bible.

Behold, I am coming soon! My reward is with me, and I will give to everyone according to what he has done. I am the Alpha *and the Omega, the First and the Last, the Beginning and the End. Blessed are those who wash their robes, that they may have the right to the tree of life and may go through the gates into the city. Outside are the dogs, those who practice magic arts, the **sexually immoral**, the murderers, the idolaters and everyone who loves and practices falsehood.* (Rev 22:12-15)

Remaining unmarried to serve God is a high calling. It was the path of Jesus. You don't have to be married to bear the image of God. We all, through mere creation, bear His image. Celibacy points to being married to God in eternity. Many in a homosexual lifestyle never seriously consider the call of God to celibacy. The opposite of homosexuality is not heterosexuality. It is holiness. Because our bodies are the blood bought temple of the Holy Spirit, a lifestyle of defiling sexual activity, including monogamous homosexuality, is not a biblical option.

Where Do We Go From Here?

Jesus' jealous desire as a Bridegroom King is to have a pure, corporate Bride at the end of history. He will not share His Bridal People with any other "god" and He will judge those who reject His covenant of love. Our race began with a wedding of a perfect Man and a perfect Woman. When we cross the finish line of history there will be a wedding with another perfect Man who has perfected another Bride with His own blood! The point of life and history is love!

Every generation fails to live up to the ideal of covenant marriage. But changing the standard is not the answer. God has taken the punishment for all covenant breakers, so we may still walk toward the Bridal City He is preparing. Until then, our part is to believe that keeping promises will reap the greatest rewards in due time. God keeps His promises and, if we are His offspring, with His help, so can we.

Finishing Life Well

Part Three

Growing a Life of Prayer

Chapter 9

Starting a Conversation with God

"Rejoice always, pray continually,
give thanks in all circumstances;
for this is God's will for you in Christ Jesus."
(1 Thess. 5:17)

What Do Guys Talk About with Girls?

If we are going to be married to God for eternity, we need to start having lots of conversation with Him now. But what does He like to talk about?

One of the biggest fears I had when going out on one of the few dates I had in high school was finding things to talk about. The more beautiful and popular the girl, the less my brain and tongue were able to function at the same time.

My place to practice the fine art of conversation with the opposite sex was while bagging groceries at the Harris-Teeter Grocery Store. There was a division of labor down gender lines. Girls ran the cash registers, while boys bagged the groceries and stocked the shelves. It was ideal for a shy kid like me. Both you and the cute girl at the register were getting paid to be there. The guy could move around, but the girl had to stick to where the money was. If business got slow and you ran out of things to talk about you could make up an easy excuse to go do something else; like get the carts in the parking lot, or straighten the cans of black eyed peas on aisle nine.

Little societies form between the male and female workers at a grocery store. Hierarchies develop. Put any group of human beings together and a pecking order will soon be established. I don't know if it is right, but it is who we are. *"Homo Hierarchicus."*

If you thought bag boys were bagging the groceries for you, you would have been mostly wrong at my store. We were bagging for the girl at the register! Bag boys at my store would compete over who got to bag groceries for which cashier. Some cashiers, based on beauty, personality, and charm never had to worry about bagging her customers' stuff.

Others? Well, life isn't fair is it? Certainly not in the world of high school teenagers with unruly hormones.

The next time you go to a grocery store and it is a bunch of high school kids working at the check out lines, don't go to the lane where the prettiest cashier is running the register. If there is a high school boy bagging behind her, there is no telling where the poor fool is going to put your loaf of bread in the bag!

So there I was, able to pretend like the prettiest cashiers in the store really enjoyed my company and lame jokes. It was good practice for a kid testing the allures and mysteries of the female psyche. I enjoyed telling a joke to the cashiers about how it was easier to know the mind of God than the mind of a woman. Here it is.

A man was given one wish by a powerful genie. "I would like you to build me a bridge from my home in California to my home in Hawaii!" he asked.

"What? That is impossible! Ask me for something else." replies the genie.

"Hmmm. Okay, I wish to understand the mind of a woman." says the man.

The genie replies, "How many lanes would you like on that bridge?"

Okay, I am not very good at telling jokes. The girls at Harris-Teeter could have told you that! For guys like me, making conversation with a being as unfathomable as a high school female was quite daunting. Sometimes, terrifying!

Somebody's Not Listening

I have a news flash for you that will make the whole enterprise of conversing with the One who made everything less daunting. This is it. He *wants* to talk with you. In fact, what I see throughout the narrative of the Bible, is that He is dying to talk to you.

I didn't always think this way. Being a preacher's kid, I talked to God a lot growing up. He never seemed to say anything back to me. I got accustomed to talking to the ceiling, or the stars, and wondering if my words went any farther. Especially after my Dad died.

I never doubted that God was real. I just knew His reality had never become real to me. I knew enough about what it meant to be a Christian to know I wasn't one. My Dad was too good of a preacher for me to be confused on that point. I did not have a personal relationship with God. But I wanted one.

I prayed for my own salvation for years before God chose to answer that prayer when I was 19 years old. Why He waited so long to break the silence, I do not know. He is God and I am not.

Without my Dad's voice, I began to do things a year after his death I never thought I would do. My Mom prayed me through those years of beer parties and passing girlfriends. One night she overheard a phone conversation I had with a friend about smoking pot that freaked us both out. I never smoked weed again after I saw how it upset Mom. I was the "man of the house" now and knew I had some changing to do. But maturity and responsibility don't hatch overnight.

I was lucky to be alive after racing my GTO through a neighborhood with a car full of beer drinking buddies on our way to re-supply the party. I obeyed their request to make the tires "bark" between every gear. The weight of a full car caused the brakes to fail as we were approaching a busy intersection with four lanes of traffic. The guys screamed with delight as I drove through a yard. They thought I was trenching it with my tires, a fairly common high school vandal's stunt. I was doing anything to avoid crossing the highway!

Their screams of fun turned to shock as I rocketed between a telephone pole and huge oak tree on the way up a grassy bank to the intersection. The next day, you could see the tracks of the car disappear in the grass as it became airborne. The tracks reappeared in the second lane. That was the spot where the gas tank dropped out from the impact of the crash landing.

Amazingly, I was able to guide the car across the rest of the lanes and "park" it on the sidewalk without hitting any traffic. My forehead was bleeding from where it hit the steering wheel when the car hit the bank. The rest of the guys were shaken up, but none of them thought it was a good idea to stick around for the police to arrive or their parents would find out about the party.

You can imagine the scene when my Mom drove up. Emergency lights of every color were flashing. Fire trucks were hosing gasoline off the street from the busted gas tank. Police cars were directing the traffic from the Elvis Presley concert that had just ended and packed the roads. And there was me sitting in the back of a cop car with blood running down my face.

I figured the blood would buy me some sympathy time with Mom until getting to the hospital for stitches. Even though the floor of my GTO reeked of spilled beers, the policeman knew I had not been drinking, which was true, thank God. But I was so busted.

God was speaking, but I wasn't listening. I wanted to listen, but I lacked the ability to hear.

"Jesus is Coming Again, You Have to Be Ready!"

My freshman year at the University of North Carolina was no better in terms of my spiritual direction in life. More alcohol, more parties, more girls, and no parents to reign me in. I lived next to a guy on our dorm floor named Mike who was a genuine follower of Jesus. I remember hearing his friends singing Christian songs through the wall and I banged on it to get them to keep it down. This was on a hall where rock music blared all the time with no complaints. Who was I becoming?

One evening right after dinner I was studying Macroeconomics and I got drowsy enough to lie down for a nap. No sooner had I dropped off, than I was awakened in a dream by my Dad. Whether it was my Dad, or Jesus, or an angel who appeared in the form of my

Dad, I can't tell you. But as far as I was concerned, *it was my Dad*. I felt like I was in an ocean of liquid love in his presence, but instinctively I knew I was not to touch him. I doubt I could have defined the word "holy" at the time. But I knew what it *felt* like in that dream.

Dad spoke to me and said, "Paul, Jesus is coming again and you have to be ready."

In my dream I said, "I'm not ready! I'm not ready!"

He said the same thing a second time, "Paul, Jesus is coming again and you have to be ready."

A second time I cried, "I'm not ready. I'm not ready."

If this wasn't enough, there were many angel voices singing over and over, "Give God the glory! Give God the glory!" while this was unfolding.

A third time my Dad says, "Paul, Jesus is coming again and you have to be ready."

I am *undone*. In my dream I am sobbing on the floor and whispering, "I'm not ready. I'm not ready." I had the audacity to ask at that point, "What about Mom?"

He answered sternly, "Your Mom is not your concern, *you* have to be ready."

Then I woke up.

Whoa. Only fifteen minutes had passed since I had closed my Macro book. I sat on the edge of the bed shaking. I got my composure back and then I wrote the dream down just in case I would ever forget. I lost that sheet of paper soon afterward, but I never forgot!

What do you do after a close encounter of the God kind? I went to the only person I thought would understand; next door to Mike's room. He and his roommate were popping popcorn, so it was normal enough for me to wander in for some hang out time. After awhile I got the courage to tell Mike the whole thing. He sat there and smiled. Mike had written me off as a preacher's kid gone wild, but that night he could see that God was pursuing me. He started getting his Christian friends to pray for me.

You'd think with a dream that powerful I would have thrown myself on the mercy of God and become a Christian on the spot. Not so. Things continued to go south spiritually for me for a year longer. I grew more and more hollow with every new experience in the party lifestyle. I wasn't miserable, but I wasn't happy either. I decided I would work at the Methodist conference grounds for the summer after my sophomore year, but *not* for the church. I did not want to be a hypocrite.

That is why the job working construction was perfect for me. And that is how I happened to be in the right spot at the right time for Lucy Downey to walk past my watching eyes!

God Uses a Pretty Face

On a dare from one of the other rednecks during our lunch break I strolled to the church office clad in my dirty T-shirt to meet the mystery woman. It was a perfect setup! The cute girl who turned every hard-hatted head worked at the Information Desk. I could just go get me some information! I know this sounds cheesy, but that is when I pretty much fell in love at first sight. After admiring a perfectly placed freckle on her cheek and thinking the name on her nametag, Lucy Downey, was the sweetest name ever, I conspired with one of her co-workers to get her to come to the Starlight Disco later that week.

Lucy nearly didn't make it. She was tired after work from giving so much information I guess. But as soon as she sat down, I sprang over to ask her to dance. The music was so loud I didn't hear her answer. It never occurred to me she would say no. Lucy doesn't remember saying yes, but it didn't matter because I had grabbed her hand and was already pulling her onto the disco floor! We got to know each other dancing to hits like "Brick House," "Disco Inferno," and "Once, Twice, Three Times a Lady." It's crazy, but people actually fell in love to those retro songs! I made a good enough impression for her to give a clear "yes" to me for a real date.

We saw a tear jerker movie, called "The Champ." Like my Dad, I would cry like a faucet during corny melodramas. Lucy was warming up to this somewhat buff construction worker who cried like a baby at the cinema. We shopped at the grocery store and I made her a meal in my basement apartment. During the evening it became apparent to her from my speech, "Uh-oh, this guy isn't a Christian!" I remember her sharing a story from her life in which her youth group bus lost its brakes coming down from the top of the Smoky Mountains National Park. Most people were panicking as glass and smoke from burning brakes was filling the speeding bus. But some of the "spirit filled" young people were praying loudly and the bus came to rest on its side in a mucky spot of grass right before a hairpin turn with a horrible drop off.

She was sharing her testimony with this lost construction worker and I was just thinking how cute she was. But something did begin to happen. After coming home from work and taking long showers in a vain attempt to get all the dirt off, I would open a Bible and start reading. I hadn't read the Bible for myself in years. I really didn't know where to start. I found myself reading in the Gospel of John and the letters of John in the New Testament. One evening in late June 1978, alone in the basement apartment, I read these words from 1 John 5:4-5:

For everyone born of God overcomes the world. This is the victory that has overcome the world, even our faith. Who is it that overcomes the world? Only he who believes that Jesus is the Son of God.

As I was reading these words, a light went on and a door opened inside of me. The words weren't just on a page, they were speaking to me. I remember looking up (Why do people always look up at moments like these?) and saying, "God I hear your voice, don't you *ever* stop talking to me!" Thirty plus years later, I can honestly say the conversation that began that day between me and God has never stopped.

A Chain of Prayers

My spiritual birth was the product of many prayers by many people. Prayers of my Dad before he died, my Mom's desperate prayers, my prayers, Mike's prayers, kids in InterVarsity Christian Fellowship's prayers, and Lucy's prayers. Those are the ones I know of.

How about you? Have you stopped to think about who is praying for you? Do you think those prayers are making a difference? Have you ever thanked people for their prayers? Do you pray for others or mostly for yourself? What do you talk about when you talk to God? If you haven't already begun, Jesus wants to start the conversation.

Chapter 10

The Power of Gratitude

"Jesus told them, 'When you pray, say:
"Father, You are Beautiful!"
(My paraphrase of Luke 11:2)

You

It is safe to say that people love to talk about themselves. Bette Midler in the old movie, "Beaches," plays a self absorbed character who was getting tired of talking about herself and says, "I've talked enough about me. What do *you* think about me?"

God actually likes to talk to you about you. He loves you more than you love yourself. He knows you better than you know yourself. His thoughts about you are better and more accurate than your thoughts about you. You would think that if anyone would be an expert on you it would be you. Wrong. God is the expert on you. You *need* to talk with Him about you and hear His voice on the subject of you.

David's song number 139, verse 17, helps us understand this idea. *"How precious concerning me are your thoughts, O God! How vast the sum of them! Were I to count them, they would outnumber the grains of sand."*

Read all of Psalm 139 to get the full effect of the intimacy of God's knowledge of each of us. It ends with David giving God permission to...*Search me, O God, and know my heart; test me and*

*know my anxious thoughts. See if there is any offensive way in me,
and lead me in the way everlasting.*

David Sang the Blues

David's language of prayer in the Psalms, the hymn book out of
the 66, is full of gut level emotional highs and lows that have comforted and inspired generations of those who would know God as
David did. If you want to see what an intimate and honest conversation with God looks like, read David's prayers. We think of them as
poems or songs, and they are. But they are a window into this man
whose greatest desire was to gaze at God's beauty 24/7.

Because so many of David's prayers were songs, we could think
of him as the original "blues" singer. He never let an emotion go to
waste. He took every ounce of gratitude and complaint and laid it
squarely in front of God. And God *loved* it!

I have a friend who loves the Blues. As a son of the South where
the Blues were born out of the moaning rhythms of slaves and their
ancestors, I enjoy a twangy blues tune myself once in a while. But
the Blues make my friend happy. Listening to how cruel life can
be, turned into a song, can lift one's soul. The Blues were exactly
that before they became a marketable genre of music. The Blues
were the sad heart song of an oppressed people. Singing them made
one more day of hard living bearable. No one can live long without
finding some happiness. We look for the silver lining of the dark
cloud. Learn to talk to God about the troubles you've seen today. He
can take it. Jesus sang the Blues on His way to the cross.

Anxiety

Have you noticed how much of our brain energy, and thus our
conversation with God, is about the things that create anxiety? Jesus
spoke directly to our anxious thoughts when He said:

*Therefore I tell you, do not worry about your life, what you will eat
or drink, or about your body, what you will wear. Is not life more
important than food and the body more important than clothes?*

Look at the birds of the air; they do not sow or reap or store away in barns, and yet your heavenly Father feeds them. Are you not much more valuable than they? Who of you by worrying can add a single hour to his life? (Matt. 6:25-27)

Don't you hear the reassuring tones of a friend's voice in those lines from the Sermon of the Mount? He is saying to us, "It's going to be *okay*."

I need to hear those words from Jesus a LOT. Most of us get worked up by the daily problems of life. Jesus isn't trying to minimize the challenges of life. He, more than any of us, knows that life is full of daily struggle, suspense, and pain. He is speaking to the deepest questions of our heart concerning whether God really knows about us, and if He is able and willing to take care of us. "Yes, yes, and yes!" comes the answer from our Bridegroom King. He has us covered.

Developing an Attitude of Gratitude

I'll be honest. I spend a lot of time talking to my Heavenly Dad about piddly, non-eternal subjects. I can just imagine Jesus telling the angel Gabriel, "Gabe, hold off on working on peace in the Middle East, Paul Hughes has lost his car keys again!"

Fortunately, it doesn't work that way! God is "undiminished" by our requests. His resources never run out and He never tires of listening. So don't hesitate to go to God with your piddly requests as well as with prayers for peace and justice in the Middle East.

Paul put it this way: "Do not be anxious for anything, but in everything, by prayer and petition, with thanksgiving, present your requests to God. And the peace of God which transcends all understanding will guard your hearts and minds in Christ Jesus." (Phil 4:6-7)

If we knew the depth of suffering Paul lived with, we would better appreciate his 24/7 attitude of praise to God. It is safe to say Paul's life was harder than ours. But he knew something about redemptive suffering that we need to press into for ourselves.

I want to know Christ and the power of His resurrection and the fellowship of sharing in His sufferings, becoming like Him in His death and so somehow, to attain to the resurrection of the dead. (Phil 3:10-11)

Jesus was given the forty lashes minus one by the Romans once. It was a horrible whipping that brought Him near the point of death. Paul received 39 lashes *five* times from his brothers the Jews because of his passion for talking about Jesus. Why wouldn't he just shut up?!

He wouldn't stay silent while suffering for Jesus, because he experienced a deep joy in sharing his suffering *with* Jesus. We need to take Paul's urging seriously. Always rejoice in the Lord! In fact, if we aren't happy in Jesus, maybe we haven't found Him yet in the hard circumstances of life and embraced our own cross behind His.

Can I Get a Witness?

When our family moved to Birmingham, Alabama from Orlando, Florida in 1998 we joined a large Black Church called Sardis Missionary Baptist Church. For most of the eight years that we were a part of the wonderful family at Sardis, we were pretty much "it" for white folk. But among the countless life lessons our family learned from years of intimate journeying in the Black community was the power of praise and thanksgiving.

I want to say this about how praise and thanksgiving can really work. I have seen it work this way once in a culturally White church for every fifty times in a culturally Black church. Somewhere in the midst of worship at Sardis, a spirit of gratitude sweeps the house. The pastor knows his people and how to bring them into a place of encounter with God. It is amazing what happens when a whole room is gripped with praise.

It isn't that we White people don't have pain and setbacks on a daily and weekly basis. We most certainly do. When we come to church we want and need to connect with God and have our spirits lifted. But there is a difference when you are part of a people whose experience in America has been 400 years of mostly oppression and "coming up the rough side of the mountain." You need a God who meets you in your situation and walks with you in the very depths of your pain. You have to know Him there for yourself.

If you are on the outside looking in to a Black prayer meeting or worship service, it might seem quaint or cliché. But let me tell you something. If you have been beat up all week and the Spirit of the Lord comes on you, you better shout. Say something!

Sometimes, the choir or preacher will hit a place in God's heart and someone in the room will just start shouting, "Thank you, Jesus! Thank you, Jesus! Thank you Jesus!" Now in some White services, that person would be a distraction, but not at Sardis. The Spirit of the Lord on that person begins to spread through hearts in the room and before you know it, that is all you can think or say, "Thank you, Jesus!"

At that point every problem, concern, lustful thought, need to check the grocery list, you name it, it is *gone*. There is nothing more real or vastly important than thanking this beautiful God-Man, Jesus, for dying on the cross when He didn't have to, but did it anyway. There is nothing that your heart wants to express more than just the simple words "Thank you, Jesus!" No current problems, or centuries of problems, matter in those ecstatic moments.

I am convinced those fleeting minutes of praise and thanksgiving are far more real in eternity than every other thought or emotion I have during the rest of the week. I wouldn't be surprised if we just spent the first eon of eternity having a Sardis Missionary Baptist Church worship service just to thank Jesus, for real, for saving our tiny little butts from a universe of sadness.

Let me tell you something. Jesus likes to be thanked. He healed ten men from leprosy one day and only one came back to thank Him. A Jewish half breed, Samaritan, no less. That guy got more than a healing, he got Jesus. How much of Jesus are we going for anyway? Do we only want what He can give us? Or do we want Him. Do we praise Him only for what He has done for us? Or do we praise Him for who He is? Both are good. One is better.

The highest praise is when we get past the laundry list of worries that He is helping us with and we get to Him. That is the place of beautiful encounter! God told father Abraham, "I am your portion and your very great reward." At the end of the day, we get GOD!

Praising God and thanking Jesus for who He is and what He has done for each of us is a basic part of the love language of prayer. We might as well get used to it now. Eternity is right around the corner. When I stand before Jesus, I already think I know what I will say to Him.

"Thank you!"

Chapter 11

God on Different Channels

"Do not put out the Spirit's fire;
do not treat prophecies with contempt.
Test everything. Hold on to the good."
(1 Thess 5:19-21)

God Still Speaks

The most amazing gift we inherit when we receive Jesus is the Holy Spirit to live inside of us. This "Third Person in the Trinity," to use the official language of the historic Church, is able to "give us the mind of Christ." The Spirit helps us carry on our conversation with God, heart to heart. Our friend Paul wrote:

God has revealed wisdom to us by His Spirit. The Spirit searches all things, even the deep things of God. For who among men knows the thoughts of a man except the man's spirit within him? In the same way, no one knows the thoughts of God except the Spirit of God. We have not received the spirit of the world but the Spirit who is from God, that we may understand what God has freely given us… We have the mind of Christ. (1 Cor 2:10-12, 16)

Later, Paul said to the same audience, "Everyone who prophesies (by the gift of the Spirit) speaks to men for their strengthening, encouragement, and comfort." (1 Cor 14:3)

In Book 66, we are told by John, "The testimony of Jesus is the spirit of prophecy."

These tidbits of scripture show us Jesus speaks by His Spirit to and through human vessels about you and me. This is the spiritual gift of "prophecy" and the main qualification is not a "charismatic" experience, but a heart of tenderness toward God and compassion for His people.

A Few Grains of Sand

One of my best friends is also my brother-in-law, Ed Hackett. Like me, Ed's life was turned completely around by another one of those Downey girls, Lucy's sister Linda. After leading a life without a clue, Ed directed prophecy teams for a community in Kansas City, Missouri where worship and prayer has been going on night and day since September of 1999. Whenever people came to receive prophetic ministry, Ed or someone like him, would explain the process of hearing from God on behalf of others. He told them about Psalm 139 and how God's thoughts about us are more numerous than the sands of all the beaches in the world. He delights to share His thoughts with those who share His heart. He will gladly give a "few grains of sand" to perfect strangers to give to one of His kids.

I have experienced this kind of ministry on several occasions. But I live with Ed on family vacations, too. God doesn't stop telling Ed things about me just because we aren't at the prayer base in KC. Ed keeps asking God for His thoughts about me and others everywhere he goes. I can't tell you how many times Ed will "get something" for other people. It is not flashy, but it sticks. Things Ed says to me are like time released capsules. Instead of fading away, the words grow stronger inside. It isn't because Ed is any different from you and me. He just constantly asks God to tell him things for those God loves and already wants to talk to. God gives him a few grains of sand. It is that simple. Of course it is off-the-charts amazing to those receiving a word from God. One true word from God is worth more than a world of false hopes.

Jesus the Prophet

Jesus disarmed people He met with information about themselves that no human source had shown Him. It wasn't a fortune telling stunt or magic trick. The way Jesus related to people "prophetically" revealed something about His *heart of friendship* for them. When He was around people He wasn't just reading minds. He was addressing the deep silent dialog of their heart. Their secret conversations with God were told to them!

Two examples are Nathanael, who became a follower of Jesus, and a Samaritan woman that Jesus met at the "water cooler" one day. "When Jesus saw Nathanael approaching, He said of him, "Here is an Israelite in whom there is nothing false."

"How do you know that about me?" Nathanael asked.

Jesus answered, "I saw you while you were still under the fig tree before Phillip called you."

Then Nathanael declared, "Rabbi, you are the Son of God; you are the King of Israel."

Jesus said, "You believe because I told you I saw you under the fig tree? You shall see greater things than that." He then added, "I tell you the truth, you shall see heaven open and the angels of God ascending and descending on the Son of Man."

Scripture as the Language of Prayer

I would love Jesus to say the same thing about me that He announced to Nathanael, wouldn't you? You are a man with a pure heart! Wow. That had to be encouraging!

"Sitting under a fig tree" was a figure of speech for someone pursuing a serious matter with God. People would sit inside the low hanging branches of fig trees for privacy. A fig tree was literally a mini-prayer room.

Nathanael was seeking God in prayer. Something about the timing of Jesus' words and Nathanael's secret thoughts connected. Then Jesus interprets the dream Jacob had thousands of years before. Remember the Stairway to Heaven? It was a dream Jacob had of angels ascending and descending on a "ladder" to Heaven where the throne of God was visible to Jacob at the top.

Jesus uses the language of the Hebrew Scriptures to connect to Nathanael's heart. In one giant step Jesus reveals that He is the Ladder that Jacob saw. Jesus is the one bringing Heaven to Earth and Earth back to Heaven. He is the "Son of Man," a term used by the wise old dreamer of the Old Testament, Daniel. Daniel used this term to describe one "like a son of man" who approached the "Ancient of Days" in one of his dreams. Are you beginning to see that God sometimes speaks to us through prophecy and dreams?

Dreams

Dreams that bring special insight from God's heart are a part of the conversation God wants to have with us, too. It took many years for Lucy and me to figure out that God was speaking to us through some of our dreams. You would think I would know that the dreams-and-visions channel existed, given my powerful dream from God before I was a believer! But the churches I attended discouraged considering dreams and other personal spiritual encounters as valid for Christians. I now see that was bad information when compared with the experiences of God's people throughout the 66 Books and the ages.

Can we go overboard with listening to our dreams? Oh yeah. But if God's passionate desire is to draw near to us in intimacy, why *wouldn't* He keep talking to us while we sleep? Some of the purest prayers I have ever prayed over my wife have been while she was snoring!

The reason I include this caveat about the language of dreams in a section about the language of Scripture and prayer is that all true personal experiences with God will resonate with the Bible. Anything we encounter that isn't in tune with the revelation of Scripture needs to be left alone. There are powerful dark spirits who would like to get inside our head, too.

The Bible Can Be Trusted

Here is a basic point. If you want to know the God of the 66 Books, you better get to know the 66 Books! That sounds like circular reasoning if there ever was. But in this case, just trust me. God inspired forty different authors of diverse walks in life to write over a period of one thousand five hundred years. Corroboration between the different authors was not possible, yet the story is coherent and compelling beyond any other.

Then God's Spirit guided others to collect those books deemed most reliable and trusted by the Bridal People themselves. He allowed the Hebrew, Greek, and Aramaic manuscripts to be preserved, organized, translated, copied, and distributed, sometimes at the cost of many human lives. Those manuscripts were externally corroborated by secular history, archeology, and scientific methods. With that much history and confirmation, we might want to read them, study them, and use the full imagery, language, thematic material, people, events, genre's, and cultures as ways to relate to the Author of it all.

I know that people are thinking the Da Vinci Code fiction or alternative gospels that have been recently "discovered" and played up on the National Geographic channel are problematic. But I can't tell you how flimsy these popular posers are compared to the historical reliability of the existing manuscripts of the Bible. No other ancient literature comes within a thousand miles of the credibility of Scripture, in spite of what your agnostic college professor is telling you.

If we are to encounter the God who has revealed Himself in history, then we must know the literature through which He has chosen to show Himself. What will you talk about with God if you do not know His life story so far?

Chapter 12

God Wants Friends

"I no longer call you servants, because a servant does not know his master's business. Instead, I have called you friends, for everything that I learned from my Father I have made known to you."
(John 15:15)

God Will Bag Your Groceries

God will talk to anybody. He doesn't mind crossing the tracks and hanging out in the "bad" part of town. For God, our whole planet is the bad part of town. Samaritans were the despised half-bred cousins of the Jews. They were not racially pure. When Jesus engaged the Samaritan woman in conversation, He broke all kinds of social rules to build a friendship. It is one of the reasons I love Jesus so much. He breaks the rules that hinder love.

Jesus tells the woman of Samaria that she has had five husbands and she is living with another man now. That opens her up to a more profound issue in her heart. She is not put off by Jesus' startlingly accurate prophetic insight. She charges forward with a burning question about the right place to worship the One true God.

"Sir," the woman said, "I can see that you are a prophet. Our fathers worshiped on this mountain, but you Jews claim the place where we must worship is in Jerusalem."

Jesus declared, "Believe me woman, a time is coming when you will worship the Father neither on this mountain nor in Jerusalem.

You Samaritans worship what you do not know; we worship what we do know, for salvation is from the Jews. Yet a time is coming and has now come when the true worshipers will worship the Father in spirit and truth, for they are the kind of worshiper the Father seeks. God is spirit, and His worshipers must worship in spirit and truth."

The woman said, "I know that Messiah (called Christ) is coming. When He comes, He will explain everything to us."

Then Jesus declared, "I who speak to you am He."

This is one power packed conversation with Jesus that can be a great example of the kind of conversation we each can have with Him now in prayer.

Like Nathanel, this woman pondered the Jewish scriptures and was eagerly looking for the Messiah to come. Her biblical understanding and inquisitive heart made this a fun conversation for Jesus, too. Jews would not allow Samaritans to come worship at their church, so they had church on their side of town on Mount Ebal. Long before Jerusalem became a center of worship, Mount Ebal was the first place God commanded the Israelites to worship in the Land He promised to bring them. This Samaritan woman knew her Bible and she went right to the major issue of that hour of history. What and where is right worship? And who will be the Messiah?

The amazing thing to me about this conversation is how much this woman is able to open up *His* heart and cause *Him* to gush with incredible revelation about true worship and even about His very identity as the Messiah. She gets clear answers to two of the biggest questions of the Ages! A hungry human heart is what turns God into a purring kitten. Jesus bagged her groceries!

What Have We Learned About Relating to God?

God wants to engage us in conversation and in friendship. He is pursuing us even when we are not pursuing Him.

He loves talking to you about you. You are one of His favorite subjects. He made you, so He has a right to enjoy you!

He is available to talk 24/7 and has more communication channels than the DISH Network.

The 66 books is the best source of ideas and language God has given us to use in our unbroken conversation with Him.

He will talk to anyone, anywhere, about anything.

God especially comes near to those who know Him for who He really is, in the good times and bad, and who praise Him with a heart of gratitude at all times.

He loves it when we learn to suffer with Him for the sake of love.

He trades His comfort and presence for our anxiety and alienation. He loves to discuss the deepest issues of our heart and answer the hardest questions of our hour of human history. True conversation with Jesus on His Throne is less expensive and more effective than a seminary education. Prayer based on the Bible is the avenue of eternal revelation.

He responds most to those who get past their own stuff and begin to ask what is on His mind for others and for the planet.

The King of the Universe is Also Your Friend

Jesus had friends. We aren't told exactly how the home of Mary and Martha and Lazarus became such a favorite place of His to unwind, but perhaps it was because it was on the way to Jerusalem. Faithful Jewish families were to go up to Jerusalem for special feast celebrations at the temple three times a year: Passover, Pentecost, and Tabernacles. It sure would have been nice to have friends in the area as close to Jerusalem as Bethany to crash with instead of staying at the Comfort Inn. Maybe they grew up knowing each other's families? It is only a theory of mine.

What we do know is that Martha, Mary, and Lazarus were close to Jesus. John specifically tells us, "Jesus loved Martha and her sister Mary and Lazarus." It was Mary who poured expensive perfume on Jesus and wiped his feet with her hair. When Lazarus was ill, the message sent to Jesus was, "Lord, the one you love is sick."

We see Jesus hanging out at their house with His disciples and Martha tries to pull Him into a fight with her sister who was far more wrapped up in listening to every word coming out of Jesus' mouth, than helping in the kitchen. I'm sure a squabble like this has never occurred at your house! He lovingly corrects Martha by saying, "Martha, Martha, you are worried and upset about many things, but only one thing is needed. Mary has chosen what is better and it will not be taken away from her." (Luke 10:41-42)

Martha is the older sister. Later, she meets Jesus first when He comes to see about Lazarus who has died. Martha tells Jesus that her brother had been dead already for four days. But she also knew that if Jesus had come earlier, he would not have died. Even so, Martha is ready to believe that Jesus may still be able to raise her brother from the dead. You get the same idea about Mary in the way she immediately runs to meet Jesus when she hears that He has sent for her.

Jesus has raised a widow's son and a synagogue leader's daughter from the dead before this, but now He is facing a situation with His dearest friends. If you read the whole scene in John's Gospel chapter 11, you can't help but see how emotionally overwhelmed Jesus is in the midst of everything. He wept deeply with them.

How much faith is necessary to see a miracle of resurrection? Jesus wanted the stone to Lazarus' tomb rolled away, but only Martha had the authority as the eldest to give the consent. She had no power to raise the dead, but she did have the authority to believe something in her own heart. A mustard seed of faith is all God needs to move a mountain or raise the dead. The stone was rolled away and Lazarus was called back to life by his friend Jesus.

In a short time, it would be Jesus walking out of a garden tomb after angels had rolled away the stone of *His* grave. Perhaps some of His tears for Lazarus were in recognition of the path He would soon be taking Himself. His friend Lazarus, like His cousin John, was a forerunner for Jesus in death.

Afterwards, at their house in Bethany, Mary senses her Lord's anguish about his own appointment with death at the hands of the powers that be in Jerusalem. Jesus had predicted his death by crucifixion in detail more than once with His disciples, but these predictions seemed to have had little real affect on them.

Not so with Mary. She took spikenard perfume worth a year's wages and poured it on Jesus in the presence of everyone, including Judas. Judas complained about the waste of money it was, but Jesus defended Mary's act of extravagant love and adoration before His burial.

Ministering to Jesus

Why have I labored to retell so much of this story? Because I want us all to see that it is possible for each one of us to "minister to Jesus" even as Mary of Bethany learned to do.

She took what she had, maybe all she had, and poured it out on this Man she loved as her Leader and Friend. She is a picture of friendship with Jesus that we can imitate. What is more, we see that it meant something to Jesus. Mary's friendship counted. It impacted Jesus. Her love for Him touched the heart of the One who was soon to die for her and her race. What looked to Judas like a terrible waste was the most perfectly timed act of worship in all of history.

What was it that Mary had that Judas didn't have? She had a heart that saw into the emotions and thoughts of her friend, Jesus. A heart of love will do that. It will cause us to see depths of reality where a selfish heart of stone will not see anything. The fears and desires of Judas and Mary couldn't have been further apart in that little house in Bethany. Soon the secret value system of their hearts would be displayed on a world stage. Both would have their stories told for generations. But the tales would be different.

There is Going to Be a Wedding!

Do you value Jesus as a friend? Do you know that there are things on His mind and emotions in His heart right now as He waits in Heaven? You can converse with Him on those themes right now. You can open your Bible like I did as a dirty construction worker and ask Him to show you what is going on in those pages. He just might do it!

Do you know that your conversation with Him can grow beyond lost car keys and the daily grind? In fact, it is your highest honor to pursue the secrets of His heart. That is the greatest pleasure of conversation with Jesus – to touch His heart. You were made to be His companion. You were made for eternal love so strong that a thousand deaths could not extinguish its desire! Talk to your Bridegroom King while He calmly runs the universe waiting to share it with you!

There is so much more to talk about with Jesus! Many of us have nothing to say unless it is to confess our sins and get forgiveness so we can feel good and go on with life. That is great, but what will we talk about in eternity when all our sins are no more? Since God has passions and desires, let's ask Him what is on *His* heart.

One woman, like Mary of Bethany, who constantly unlocks the heart of Jesus is a singer, songwriter, and worship leader named Misty Edwards. Her lyrics come from decades of dialoging with Jesus. Where has the language of her prayer life gone? "Jesus, here I am Your favorite one! What are You thinking? What are you feeling? I have to know!" Misty gets *tons* of bagged groceries!

Do we have any idea how patiently Jesus waits for His Bride to match His passion? He wants to consummate the Marriage with us! The crescendo at the end of the Bible is a choral duet of the Holy Spirit and the Bride of Christ crying out "Come! King Jesus, come!"

On His Wedding Day, Jesus gets the Bride of His dreams and His Father gets the honor He deserves as the coolest Dad ever. All of the angels will marvel at the sheer wonder and wisdom of God's ways. The creation that groans for this Day to come will burst forth with clapping trees and singing mountains!

In John 17:24, Jesus is talking to His Father in the vulnerable hours before His suffering for the Bride He is to cleanse with His blood. What is *Jesus'* "One Thing Desire?

Father I desire those you have given me to be with me where I am, and to see my glory, the glory you have given me, because you loved me before the creation of the world.

That is Jesus' greatest desire! For us who love Him to be with Him in the Presence of His Father forever! He is enjoying the long phone conversations, but He wants to finally get married!

Finishing Life Well

Part Four

The Relay Race of Faith

Chapter 13

Cheers Beyond the Finish Line

"Therefore, since we are surrounded by such a great cloud of wit-
nesses, let us throw off everything that hinders and the sin that so
easily entangles, and let us run with perseverance
the race marked out for us." (Heb 2:1)

A Tradition of Finishing Well

I am a product of the Tar Heel State. Few things were more exciting to me growing up than the glorious game of basketball. In North Carolina, we had a choice of four colleges in the Atlantic Coast Conference that played the game with national excellence each year. In some years, NC State had the best team. Other years, Wake Forest would be the team to beat among the Big Four. Then there was Duke, or "Dook," as everyone who was not a "Dookie" spelled it. No disrespect intended of course. "Not!!" And then there was Carolina. Ahh yes, the University of North Carolina would eventually win the sweepstakes of my affections.

Even though my Dad was a Dookie, I went to Carolina, and as fate would have it, I lived on the floor just beneath where all the UNC basketball players lived. It was a big rush for my little ego to party with Walter Davis, a future NBA Rookie of the Year. I once played pinball with another NBA player-to-be, Mike O'Koren. The sound coming through my ceiling of Al Wood bouncing basketballs

115

was music to my ears. I was blessed to live so near the basketball gods!

Sure it was a vicarious life. I was a pimply face in the crowd. But what a crowd! I rocked with the student section in the old Carmichael Auditorium as the Carolina hoopsters performed their aerial feats. Just being close to such talent and fame and mythical basketball tradition was a religious experience. Hanging from the ceiling in Carmichael were banners of championship teams and retired jerseys of some of the greatest players in the Carolina Blue pantheon. The tradition of excellence was something you could feel in the air.

In the spring of my freshman year in 1977, the Tar Heels went all the way to the NCAA Championship Game against Marquette. After every tournament win there were post game celebrations of increasing intensity. I remember running with a spontaneous stampede of students across the whole campus. Our momentum carried us through the library shouting to all the people studying that the Tar Heels had won another game.

I may never run with the bulls through the streets of Pamplona, Spain, but I have run through Franklin Street in downtown Chapel Hill with crazed Tar Heel fans. I doubt there would have *been* a downtown if we had won the title that year. There was still a celebration on Franklin Street after the championship loss to Marquette. Only a few cars and other property were destroyed. I would never experience a National Championship as a student. I graduated in the spring of 1980. That fall, a freshman named Michael Jordan arrived. Two years later, he would hit a title winning shot that would really spark some damage on Franklin Street.

God's Hall of Fame

Does Jesus care about ACC basketball? According to Wake Forest fans, whose mascot is a demon possessed church deacon, yes! Their saying was, "If God is not a Demon Deacon, why is the Bible black and gold?" That was, of course, their school colors.

That motto was a spin-off from the Carolina claim that, "If God is not a Tar Heel, why is the sky Carolina blue?"

I seriously doubt when we bow before Jesus on His Day, that we will kiss His "Air Jordan" basketball shoes. He has His own hall of fame. They are the saints. It isn't only saints in the sense of men and women so designated by the official church hierarchy. *Everyone* who belongs to Jesus is a saint. The word literally means *owned*. He bought us with His blood. The saints of the Bible are those whose lives stand out because of one quality. Faith.

Aren't you glad that God's evaluation of us at the end of the day isn't based on how well we can dunk a basketball, pass an academic exam, or build a mega-church empire? Our standing is based on one thing. In Galatians 5:6, Paul says, "The only thing that counts is faith working through love." When we stand before Jesus, He will ask "How much did you learn to know and trust Me?" That hits all of us right in the kisser. We can't pass the buck. Each of us is accountable to God for the quality of trust in our own heart in our own world. Do *I* have faith in God and in His promises to *me*?

Scholars of the Bible aren't sure about who wrote the New Testament book of Hebrews. But whoever did write it did a good thing, especially in chapter eleven. That chapter has been nick-named "The Hall of Faith." Verse six says, "Without faith it is impossible to please God." Wow. Really amazing deeds done from out of our own desires apart from trust in God amount to zero. They may impress men, but not God. God is moved by our response of "Yes!" to His character and leadership.

There were a whole bunch of folks who lived with a "yes" in their hearts toward God before you and I got here. They finished well. Their jerseys are retired in Heaven. We ought to imitate their lives.

The Hall of Faith

First on the list is Abel, the second born son of Adam and Eve. Abel brought God a better sacrifice than his older brother Cain. Which is interesting since Abel's name means "nothing" or "meaningless" and Cain means, "I have gotten a man". Eve was wrong in her perception about which of her boys would carry the hopes for a future son who would bring God the most pleasing sacrifice ever.

In one act of jealousy, Cain disqualified himself and murdered Abel. Now what will Eve do? Little Seth comes later.

Abel is God's way of saying to us that the "nobody" playing second fiddle can please him by the quality of their faith toward Him. Abel's act of adoration pleased God. He is the first in what is called the "cloud of witnesses." The text says that Abel "still speaks, even though he is dead."

That is the essence of the lives of those who have finished life well before us. Their lives still speak to us. When each has run his race of faith and finished well in death (except in Enoch's case when God just took him alive and kicking to heaven) they join the rest of the cloud of others who have done the same. Noah, Abraham, Sarah, Isaac, Jacob, Joseph, Moses, Rahab, Gideon, Barak, Samson, Jepthah, David, Samuel, and the prophets are mentioned in Hebrews 11.

We are told these men and women "were still living by faith when they died. They did not receive the things promised; they only saw them and welcomed them from a distance ...They were longing for a better country — a heavenly one. Therefore God is not ashamed to be called their God, for He has prepared a city for them."

They were not living the "blessed life" of faith and prosperity sold as a commodity for a donation on some TV programs that teach a different kind of faith message. Our forerunners in the relay race of faith were tortured, jeered, flogged, stoned, sawn in half, and barely clothed. They were destitute, wanderers, mistreated, and homeless. These are the kind of heroes we are exhorted to be like as Hebrews chapter twelve begins.

The Cloud of Witnesses

Therefore since we are surrounded by such a great cloud of witnesses, let us throw off everything that hinders and the sin that so easily entangles, and let us run with perseverance the race marked out for us. Let us fix our eyes on Jesus, the author and perfecter of our faith, who for the joy set before Him endured the cross, scorning its shame, and sat down at the right hand of the throne of God.

Consider Him who endured such opposition from sinful men, so that you will not grow weary and lose heart. (Hebrews 12:1-3)

I inherited a bed from my grandparent's home that some of my ancestors were born and died in. While telling my youngest son about the bed I said, "Daniel, I bless you with the blessing of your forefathers and foremothers!" He got a twinkle in his eye and asked coyly, "Where are my other three fathers and three mothers, Dad?" We all have forefathers in our legacy of faith. Probably more than just "four" fathers! You have a faith family tree even if it isn't your natural forefathers. Abraham is the father of us all if we have faith in God. We are adopted into a great Household of Faith when we join the forever family of God.

Be encouraged by the cloud of witnesses in the Bible and in the lives of saints who finished well throughout history. Biographies and journals of great women and men of God have powerfully influenced how I follow Jesus. Great faith is the ability to persevere through trials and not take our eyes off Jesus. It is far more than a sanctified wish list of vocational goals or things you want God to add to your life.

I have never been a farmer, but I am told that it was not easy in the old days to plow a straight furrow. If you looked down in front of you, you would zig and zag without even knowing it. The trick was to fix your gaze on a certain fence post or tree across the field and march straight for it. Jesus is our fixed reference point in the race of faith. His life speaks and keeps us moving in a straight path to where He is waiting. His Spirit lives in us to empower us for every step of our own faith journey.

Do you have family members or friends who finished their life of faith well? We all need examples of people we know who kept their eyes fixed on Jesus and finished well. They are waiting across the finish line, cheering us on!

Chapter 14

Welcome to My Cloud – Part One

"(God) is not the God of the dead,
but of the living, for to Him all are alive." (Luke 20:38)

Sometimes the Veil of Heaven is Thin

I had a spiritual encounter at the end of 21 days of prayer and fasting at our church, Fullness Christian Fellowship, in Birmingham, AL in January of 2007. It was Sunday morning and suddenly in the midst of the worship one-by-one, certain people from my "faith family tree" began to appear and form a heavenly delegation around me.

First it was my Dad who came smiling and stood on my left. Then Jack Arnold, our pastor in our Florida days, came and stood on my right. Then Sequoia and Junaluska of the Ani-Kituhwa-gi (or Cherokee). Then Stacey Woods and Bill Bright, the founders of two significant campus ministries in the US. Then Francis Asbury, the first Bishop of the American Methodist Church. Then Christy Wilson, the first director of the Urbana Mission Conventions and pioneer Christian worker serving Muslim people in Central Asia. And then Martin Luther King, Jr. and an old friend and campus ministry colleague, Alex Anderson.

Ten great men of faith in my personal history in multi-generational ways were standing around me! Each in unique ways represented a spiritual legacy that I had inherited. I was serving a purpose of God in my generation that they had served in theirs. They put their hands on my shoulders and blessed me. It was all done silently. There were no voices, only smiles.

I was so amazed by what was happening, I pondered it for days before I told Lucy. Was this more than the Holy Spirit speaking through my imagination? Was this an experience of the communion of the saints that Bridal People affirm in the Apostle's Creed? Was there some sense in which these men were actually there with me? Why these ten men? Why at this time in my life?

I don't have answers to all these questions, but I do believe something. Sometimes the veil between those of us who are still running our race and those who have finished theirs is thin. I believe the veil was very thin for me that morning.

Jesus said His Dad was not the God of the dead, but of the living. Those who are dead to us are alive to Him. (Luke 20:38)

In commenting on the way in which God works through generations through faith, Jesus wasn't endorsing ancestor worship, saint worship, voodoo, or consulting the dead through mediums or witchcraft. These are things the Bible clearly forbids. He was affirming that there is One Father and One Covenant Faith Family. The promises of God made to our spiritual forefathers and foremothers are active in every succeeding generation as we receive the gift of faith from God to walk in the same Spirit they lived in. God's Spirit causes us to trust His promises from the past that only find their fulfillment in the Age to come.

By faith, Abraham obeyed when he was called to go to the place which he would receive as an inheritance. He went out not knowing where he was going. By faith he dwelt in a land of promise as in a foreign country, dwelling in tents with Isaac and Jacob, the heirs of the same promise; for he was looking forward to a city with foundations, whose architect and builder is God. (Hebrews 11:8-10)

We, like Isaac and Jacob inherit the Bridal Covenant through the work of Jesus on the cross when He made One New Man out of Jew and Non-Jew. (Eph. 2:14-16) We share the very same promise and future God gave them. We live as strangers in this world and in this Age. We are passing through on our way to an inheritance that we will share with future generations of those who will also share in this promise. "All of God's promises are 'Yes' and 'Amen' in Jesus!" (2 Cor. 1:20) Jesus has fulfilled some of the marriage vows God made to His Bridal People at the Cross, but He is returning to fulfill the rest of God's promises in the future.

Even though God's People today have more of the redemptive story revealed through human history than those heroes of Hebrews 11, we, like Abraham, are still looking forward to the Bridal City. "For here we have no enduring city, but we seek the one to come." (Hebrews 13:14)

Abraham and his sons lived in tents. Tents are mobile and temporary. They dreamed of the future city God would build that would be permanent. Without even realizing it, Abraham would offer Isaac as a sacrifice on the very place, Mount Moriah, where Solomon's temple would be built in that very city of longing - Jerusalem! When we simply walk by faith in our Father, not knowing how things will actually turn out, we sow seeds of eternity that future generations reap.

It wasn't until I began writing this book months after the experience with ten of my spiritual forefathers that it seemed that I should ask God to give me more understanding as to how their lives "still speak." for the sake of a broader audience.

I know some of these men are well known to many readers and others to only a few. But each have a historical or spiritual connection to the race of faith I am still running. I offer these vignettes in a way that I hope will illustrate how each of us has a Hall of Faith that inspires us on a particular track to finish our life and part of history well.

I invite you to think about the kind of spiritual contribution or inheritance you have received from your faith family. How are their lives still speaking to you? What prayers did they pray that are yet unanswered that might be part of the legacy you have inherited? In turn, what prayers can you pray that others will receive as assignments after your race is run? Life in God is a relay race. Don't drop the baton. Pass it on!

Welcome to My Cloud

All of the men who stood with me on January 21, 2007 were known to have been followers of Jesus. I have already told you some things about my Dad, but let me tell you a little bit more.

Bubba

Like so many sons of the South, my Dad, Miles Preston Hughes, Jr. was affectionately known as "Bubba" to his family. One of the things about my Dad that I was always proud of later in life was how he was a preacher of righteousness in Alabama during the days of racial segregation. I have all his sermon records from 1946 onward. Every year he would preach on the brotherhood of the races.

In 1955, things were getting tense in the South as the Black community was beginning to rise up in protest. My Dad stood firm for racial equality. Certain influential people in his church at First Methodist in Montevallo, AL did not like his stand on the race issue and put pressure on the Bishop to move him. My Dad moved our family to North Carolina to be in a more racially progressive state. That is why I was born there instead of Alabama like the rest of my siblings. When God called Lucy and me from Florida to Alabama in 1998, we wound up living in the Birmingham suburbs of Shelby County, the same county from which my Dad and family moved in 1956. When Lucy and I moved here it was to take up an old family legacy in a new generation.

Before moving, my Dad set an example for his younger brother, Bob, who was also a Methodist minister in Alabama. Bob's outspokenness for peaceful integration of public schools as decreed by the landmark Brown vs. the Board of Education 1954 Supreme Court case got him appointed by Bishop Clare Purcell to lead a race relations organization later called the Alabama Council on Human Relations. It was funded by the Ford Motor Foundation out of Detroit. My Uncle Bob asked another young minister in Montgomery, Martin Luther King, Jr., to be vice-president. I will return to Bob's story later. He and my Aunt Dottie are still living, so they aren't in the cloud yet!

Jack Arnold

For eleven years Dr. Jack Arnold was our pastor at a small Presbyterian Church (PCA) in Winter Park, FL. Jack was a character bigger than life! He and his wife Carol were students at UCLA back in the very first days of Campus Crusade for Christ. They both were among the first students to become followers of Jesus in the living room of founders Bill and Vonette Bright. Jack played basketball for famed UCLA coach, John Wooden, before the dynasty years, mostly "riding the pine" on the bench.

Jack was a passionate student and teacher of God's word. He was a graduate of Dallas Theological Seminary and won the Systematic Theology award. I spent many early mornings with a few other men at his home for prayer. He was a father, mentor, and friend to me. Unlike most Presbyterian pastors who are Amillennial in their view of end times, Jack was still respected by his peers for his strong Historic Premillennial view of scripture. He taught Church Polity at the Reformed Theological Seminary in Orlando.

Jack stepped down from his pulpit in 1997 to travel the world and start a ministry to train third world pastors. His best years were his last. He and Carol would go to the most primitive places around the globe to equip pastors and their wives.

We always knew that Jack would die with his boots on. Boy did he! He was filling the pulpit back at Covenant Presbyterian on January 9, of 2005. The sermon theme verse that day was also Jack's life verse, "For me to live is Christ, to die is gain!" He preached with his typical great enthusiasm with veins popping from his forehead. Only today, he preached himself right into the arms of Jesus. It was shocking for those there that Sunday morning. It isn't everyday that the minister enters heaven before the sermon is over.

According to elder Mike Beatis, who was present that morning, "Jack had just quoted John Wesley, who said, 'Until my work on this earth is done, I am immortal. But when my work for Christ is done...' and then Jack slapped his hands together and pointed towards the sky saying, 'I am outta here! I don't know about you, but when my work is done, I will go to be with Jesus. And that will be *gain*! And when I go to heaven...'

At this point Jack paused briefly, looked up, swayed slightly and grabbed the podium before falling back to the floor. Jack suffered a total cardiac arrest. He was gone.

Jack was given a precious death. He always wanted to be famous. His death while preaching made national news. Carol and others are carrying on Jack's work around the world. God buries His workers, but His work goes on.

Junaluska

Lake Junaluska in Haywood Co, North Carolina is where I met the two most important people in my life, Lucy Downey and Jesus of Nazareth, in June 1978. This picturesque mountain lake village is also the convention grounds of the United Methodist Church in the Southeastern US. The Lake was named for Cherokee leader Gul'Kala'Ski Tsu-Mu-La-Hun-Ski, or Junaluska, as White people called him. A statue of Junaluska stands in front of the main auditorium today.

My ancestors and all later arrivals in this nation are indebted to the First Immigrants who welcomed us to this land. Most Native Americans helped us survive instead of killing us when we were most vulnerable. My family story and our national story are interwoven with that of First Nations People.

Samuel Hughes brought his family down the Blue Ridge from Pennsylvania along with many other Scotch/Irish/Welsh settlers at the end of the 1700's. He settled in the beautiful heart of Cherokee Country along the Pigeon River in what was to become Haywood Co. He and his wife eventually crowded eight children into the primitive homestead carved out of the woods. The Cherokee mother village, Kituhwa, from which all modern Cherokee peoples descended, was not far away. In 1802, my great-great-grandfather, Gabriel, was born.

Gabriel would leave North Carolina to go with his brother, Joseph, to Dahlonega, GA during the gold rush that began in 1828. As the gold rush played out, Gabriel and Joseph went west to Alabama in 1839 and settled at a little place called Double Springs near the Coosa River. It was near the remains of Turkeytown, the largest Cherokee town in North Alabama. The federal removal of the Cherokee had occurred just a year before. In 1846 Gabriel and Joseph and a friend would establish the city of Gadsden, Alabama. It was named for James Gadsden, an Indian fighter and US senator whose lobbying for railroad routes for the pre-Civil War South helped get Gadsden on the map. The present US-Mexico border between El Paso, Texas, and Yuma, Arizona is the result of the Gadsden Purchase for a southern transcontinental railway.

Junaluska lived near my ancestors in North Carolina. He would also travel to Alabama, but it would be to fight a war. Messengers from Shawnee leader Tecumseh came to Soco Gap in North Carolina to rally Native tribes in war against the United States. Many Cherokee wanted to fight. But Junaluska swore that he would never lift his arm against the White Man. He helped muster one hundred Cherokee warriors to join Andrew Jackson's troops to fight against a faction of the Creek Indians who did join Tecumseh.

Junaluska's leadership under fire against the Red Stick Creeks at the Battle of Horseshoe Bend in Alabama in 1814 was a key to turning the tide of the conflict. More than eight hundred Creek warriors and their families were killed and mutilated. Less than forty Americans and their Indian allies were lost. It was the single greatest loss of Indian lives in a military engagement between the US Army and Native peoples in our country's history. Junaluska is credited with saving the life of the young General Jackson who later rode the fame of Horseshoe Bend to the White House.

In a stunning act of betrayal, partly motivated by the Dahlonega gold rush on Cherokee land, President Jackson ignored the ruling of the US Supreme Court (which upheld the land rights of Indians) and decreed the Indian Removal Act of 1830. It was one of the most far reaching unjust decisions ever made by our country. It set the stage for decades of horrible mistreatment of Native peoples. What White Americans remember as "Manifest Destiny," the sense of God-ordained White European settlement from coast to coast, most Native Americans remember as genocide.

The man Junaluska helped save in Alabama in 1814 forcibly removed him and his people in 1838 from their beautiful mountain homeland and made them march to Oklahoma during one of the coldest winters ever recorded. More than one quarter of the 16,000 Cherokee who began the march died on the "Trail of Tears." Junaluska survived the removal west and was allowed by the North Carolina Legislature to return home to the Snowbird Mountains, walking all the way. He was given 100 acres and is buried in Robbinsville near the Tennessee border. When I prayed at Junaluska's grave I felt the legacy of his heart for friendship. I did not feel unforgiveness toward Andrew Jackson. As far as I know Andrew Jackson was also a man of passionate faith in Jesus.

I later prayed at Fort Jackson near Wetumpka, Alabama. It was there in 1814 that General Andrew Jackson signed the treaty that forced the Creek and Cherokee nations to cede millions of acres of their lands as war reparations to the United States after the Battle of Horseshoe Bend. The Holy Spirit had me pray from James 2 that day. "Brothers, do not hold the faith of our Lord Jesus Christ, the Lord of Glory, with partiality... If you really fulfill the royal law according to scripture, 'You shall love your neighbor as yourself,' you do well; but if you show partiality, you sin."

Is there anything that Christian descendents today can do to right the past wrongs of their forefathers? Yes. The blood of Jesus covers all our sins, past, present, and future. First we must recognize that we are one in the Body of Christ despite our differences. Then we must honor one another as coheirs in the Kingdom of God. All Kingdom relationships must begin with a sense of the fatherhood of God and the brotherhood of man. We are one because of the blood covenant we share through the death of Jesus.

Sometimes that blood covenant requires specific acts of restoration by one generation for the sins of forefathers.

On February 22, 2006, God called me to a fifty day "Jubilee Fast". He showed me the face of a Cherokee brother in Christ, Randy Woodley. I heard a verse I later discovered was Jeremiah 8:11, "Why do you treat the wound of my people as if it were not serious?" Jesus was challenging me to do something to heal the wound in the Native heart.

I got Lucy's blessing to travel to see Randy in Kentucky where he had established a Native American training center in the tradition of L'bri. (L'bri was a transformational learning center in the Swiss Alps founded by the late Dr. Francis Schaeffer.) Randy's Eloheh Village for Indigenous Leadership and Ministry Development was where God gave me the theme for this book. I sat on a stump near a stream and felt the Lord prompting, "Ask me for anything." I waited quietly for the desire of my heart to surface. I knew whatever I asked would be given. What did I ask of the Lord?

"I want to finish well," I whispered.

Nearly six years later, that is still my heart's cry. God continues to take me on a journey into the future by discovering more of the past. Land, history, and creation itself is healed and restored through acts of honor by you and me. No righteous act is too small. No one but God may ever even know they were done.

The sixty-plus descendents of my Gabriel Hughes family line sold our last 115 acres in Gadsden in December of 2010. Lucy and I had a plan for our portion. We gave all of our inheritance to Randy as a way to honor the Cherokee who had once cared for the land before my people came.

It was also during that month that several of my praying friends were repenting for the sins of the first European to visit Alabama. Rancher Miles Albright, the leader of a "Cowboy Church" near Huntsville, Alabama was intrigued with the length of time when Israel left the Promised Land for Egypt under Jacob and when Israel returned to the Promised Land under Joshua. It was 470 years. Miles counted back from 2010 to 1540, but he had no idea what significance that year held until he found a book his wife left open about Spanish exploration of the New World on the coffee table.

In 1540, the Spanish Conquistador Hernando de Soto would bring much sorrow and death to the Native people of the North American Southeast. Miles felt like Alabama was somehow entering into a season of promise similar to how Israel did when coming back into their inheritance. I remembered the amount of the check we sent to Randy. $1,540. In that moment, God whispered to my heart, "The debt of 1540 has been paid."

Many prophetic promises have been spoken over Alabama which the intercessors and leaders of God's people are pressing into. I believe in the coming years we will see cities transformed by the power of God through a bold, praying, humble, and unified Church in the heart of the South. May it be so, Jesus.

I also believe that in the Age to come there will be a restoration of lands and godly inheritances in the spirit of Israel's Year of Jubilee. All of God's children will have a piece of heaven on earth. I believe it will not only be the Jews who have an ancient homeland restored, but all people will enter a restful inheritance of some kind in the Millennial Kingdom to come.

Sequoia

Toyota trucks are named for him. High tech businesses and ancient mighty trees are as well. Born in Tennessee, Sequoia lived in Northeast Alabama for a while before he also fought with Jackson's army against the Red Stick Creeks at Horseshoe Bend.

He was a crippled, half-breed Cherokee, who was ridiculed by his own people before revealing the reason for his years of isolation. Sequoia created something that no other illiterate person, or person period for that matter, had ever done. He created a written language by himself!

Sequoia's "syllabary" contained 86 symbols that had every sound in the complex Cherokee tongue. It was adopted in 1821 by the Cherokee Nation; and by 1825, the new syllabary had been used to translate the Bible and hymnbooks. He "voluntarily" moved to Oklahoma before the removals of 1838-39. The place where he completed the syllabary later became a concentration camp during the Indian removal in 1838, Ft. Payne, Alabama.

It is no wonder that another Cherokee Chief, Yonaguska (Drowning Bear), once said of the Bible, "It is a good book – strange that the White People are not better, after having had it so long."

The story of God's Bridal People in America is still being written. We as European-descended followers of Jesus need to become aware of the often desperate conditions of Native peoples in our country. We need to listen to their pain and serve their needs. We also need to honor their stories and way of living. We need to know each other and love each other as friends. It is long overdue.

Chapter 15

Welcome to My Cloud - Part Two

"These were all commended for their faith, yet none of them received what had been promised, since God had planned something better for us so that only together with us would they be made perfect." (Hebrews 11:39-40)

Francis Asbury

Asbury was born near Birmingham, England in 1745. He responded to a call from John Wesley, the founder of Methodism, to go as a missionary to America. He was one of two British men who left for the Colonies in 1771. He never saw his family or England again.

He was ordained in Baltimore during the "Christmas Conference" of 1784 as the first Bishop of American Methodism. Asbury helped Methodism become the fastest growing American Christian movement of the late 1700's and early 1800's. He rode over 260,000 miles crisscrossing the new nation from New England to South Carolina and buried nine horses in the process.

Averaging a sermon a day over his 45 years of ministry, Asbury preached Jesus Christ wherever he went, planting churches and installing other horseback circuit rider Methodist preachers all over pioneer America. His journals are an amazing account of someone whose passion for Jesus is unparalleled. The hardships Asbury endured from the elements on his horseback treks are a miracle in themselves. He preached anywhere: a widow's rented room, a tavern, a cabin as filthy as a stable, an orchard, a paper mill, a crowd at a public hanging, a wagon carrying men to their execution. When many Methodist clergy left America during the Revolutionary War, Asbury remained – and never renounced his British citizenship. Perhaps no one did more to bring the gospel of Jesus Christ to a new nation.

There is a decent chance that my Hughes ancestors heard Asbury preach when he came through Haywood County in November of 1810 and stayed with Jacob Shook. We know the Hughes' became Methodists and lived nearby. I have stood in the 3rd story attic chapel where Asbury preached in the Shook house which is now a museum in Clyde, NC. Long before there were any church buildings for the pioneers, people gathered to worship in homes, barns, or under the trees for "camp meetings." Gabriel would have been eight years old. Did he become a follower of Jesus directly through Francis Asbury? Perhaps.

What I do know is that when my great-great-grandfather, Gabriel helped found the town of Gadsden, Alabama in 1846, he gave the land for the First Methodist Church to be built. Later, the North Alabama Conference of the Methodist Church would be founded there. This same conference would be the one that my Dad and his little brother, Bob, would be a part of when they became pastors, three generations later. It would also be the same conference, dripping with racism, that would drive them *out* of Alabama during the Civil Rights movement.

Methodism in America has a great legacy. In 2008, I stood in the Lovely Lane Methodist Church in Baltimore founded by Asbury as the "Mother Church of American Methodism." I prayed that the revival Spirit that birthed the early Methodist movement would again transform our nation in the spirit of Francis Asbury.

Bill Bright and Stacey Woods

I only met Bill Bright, the founder of Campus Crusade for Christ, once. He came to hear his friend and spiritual son, Jack Arnold, preach and I was leading worship that day. I worked for InterVarsity

Christian Fellowship which had too often had an uneasy relationship with Campus Crusade. Both were powerful evangelical college campus ministries, but across the decades there was sometimes competition and jealousy instead of unity and respect between the organizations.

As the North and Central Florida Area Director for InterVarsity, I was the point person on the ground when Dr. Bright chose to move the whole massive Crusade headquarters from Southern California to Orlando in the early 1990s.

Soon after the move to Orlando, Dr. Bright was gripped by a passion for fasting and prayer. He had a vision for 2 million believers fasting and praying for 40 days. I was a part of the first of several gatherings he hosted in Orlando for leaders all across America as he issued this call. I have since been given grace on several occasions to fast and pray over long periods of time like Dr. Bright. I honor him for his influence in my life in an area that has benefited me greatly in my walk with Christ.

Dr. Bright developed some serious health issues but finished well, influencing the next generation of world changers from his bedside as his strength faded. One of those was a prayer leader named Mike Bickle, who would be used of God to found the International House of Prayer in Kansas City, Missouri. I would pray for Dr. Bright twice a day as I passed his condo in downtown Orlando on my commute to and from the InterVarsity office.

C. Stacey Woods was an Australian born in 1909 who, after being educated at Wheaton College and Dallas Theological Seminary, became the General Secretary of InterVarsity Christian Fellowship in Canada at the age of 25! In 1939, he crossed the border to begin pioneering IVCF-USA, also serving as its General Secretary. If that wasn't enough, Stacey Woods would help organize and found the International Fellowship of Evangelical Students (IFES) in 1947 and serve as its first General Secretary. Today there are national student movements in about 150 nations that are associated through the IFES.

Lucy and I have helped to pioneer IFES campus movements in Latvia, Ukraine, and Tajikistan. But perhaps our most personal connection to Stacey is through the family of the Chicago businessman who was Stacey's friend and the Chairman of InterVarsity's Board for its first ten years. Herbert J. Taylor's wisdom, generosity, and close friendship with Stacey were essential to launch InterVarsity.

After moving to Birmingham in 1998, through blind circumstances, I met Herbert J. Taylor's grandson who lives near the city. Al Mathis continued in his Granddad's spirit by serving as our first chairman on the board for Kingdom Forerunners. Not only that, but Al is the owner of DeSoto Caverns near Birmingham where Hernando de Soto visited in 1540. Al is descended from the Royal Hapsburg family line. His relative, King Charles the fifth of Spain, commissioned de Soto's expedition for gold and conquest to North America. It is Al Mathis who has had the authority in his lineage to repent for the sins of Hernando de Soto and his dark legacy across the Southeastern states.

Sometimes we discover how our family legacies give us a grace to speak to current realities with authority. Al and I are discovering something even more unusual. Our family lines are interconnected on multiple levels for the sake of healing the land and ushering in spiritual transformation under the leadership of Jesus.

Al and I, like Bill Bright and Stacey Woods, love how praying college students change the world.

Dr. Bill Bright and C. Stacey Woods both pioneered Christian campus movements around the world. I honor both men and look forward to eternity with them. Through InterVarsity Christian Fellowship and Campus Crusade for Christ, Stacey and Bill are still changing the world!

Dr. Christy Wilson

Christy Wilson directed the first of the student missionary conventions hosted by InterVarsity in Toronto in 1946. Over the decades this gathering has inspired hundreds of thousands of collegians to take the message and mission of Jesus to the waiting world. One such student was Jim Elliott, from Wheaton College, who was speared with four other friends in the jungles of Ecuador on January 8, 1956 as they sought to reach the remote native people there. Their deaths became world news and their courageous wives, like Jack Arnold's wife, carried on their labor of love.

I did briefly meet Dr. Wilson at Urbana 1996. The next time I would see his face was in a very surprising place. He died in 1999. But his picture was hanging on a wall in a camp along the Varzob River in the mountains above Dushanbe, Tajikistan. I was there in 2005 leading a weekend retreat for Christian and Muslim Tajik college students investigating Jesus. What a joy to have all our meetings in a room where Christy's smiling face looked on!

Dr. Wilson was a seminary professor after serving for 22 years in Afghanistan. He loved the people of Central Asia and helped introduce Afghans to Jesus. Christy also mentored a man named Arch Davis who is a brilliant Princeton University alumnus and friend of our family.

I met Arch at a gathering of 10,000 young adults at the One Thing Conference in Kansas City in 2004. He wanted me to know that Christy (who became a friend of Vineyard Church founder John Wimber) would have loved the One Thing movement. So even though the One Thing Conference gathers in Kansas City between Christmas and New Years Day at the same time as the Urbana Conference in St. Louis on the other side of Missouri, prayers of blessing are prayed for one another from both platforms.

In 2006, "Urbana" moved from Illinois to St. Louis right next to the Gateway Arch Memorial to Westward expansion. When constructed in 1965 this huge, graceful parabola rose as both "legs" were built. The nation watched to see if the last and smallest piece would drop into place to connect the two legs. Would the engineers get their math right? It fit!

I believe "Arch" Davis was a voice confirming that the Urbana and One Thing young adult gatherings along Interstate 70 were two massive worship and mission legs standing together, like the Gateway Arch, with Jesus as our capstone! Praying for each other connects us in Jesus and helps us get our spiritual math right. There is another great expansion of the Kingdom of God taking place right now through a global army of praying young adults. As we pray and speak life over one another I believe we will see a sprint to the global finish line.

Christy Wilson is still smiling!

Dr. Martin Luther King, Jr.

Most of the planet knows of Martin Luther King, Jr. I have toasted his memory with Muslim university leaders on the other side of the world. But I know him best through a couple of people who were directly part of the community and movement he inspired.

Who knew this bright young Baptist preacher fresh from Atlanta would become known all over the world as a "drum major for justice"? My Uncle Bob chuckles now, but in late 1954 he asked his ministry peer, Martin, to serve as the vice-chair of the Montgomery Council on Human Relations. Martin Luther King, Jr. readily agreed.

Martin joined the Alabama Council on Human Relations with several others including Rosa Parks and her Mom, Rev. Ralph Abernathy, and white ministers including Bob Graetz. They met for monthly bi-racial dialog and called meetings. This was before Rosa's act of defiance in not giving up her seat on a Montgomery Bus provided the spark that gave rise to the whole national Civil Rights movement.

God ordained the birth of the American Civil Rights Movement in the hearts of followers of Jesus Christ. In the early days of mass meetings in "Negro" churches across "Old Dixie" it was in the place of ecstatic worship and prayer, and powerful Bible based preaching, that a vision of God's Kingdom motivated a tired oppressed African-descended population to suddenly gain hope for a brighter future in America.

The term coined for the movement was, "The Beloved Community." The Kingdom of Jesus and the social ethic he preached from the Sermon on the Mount was the inspiration behind the term. A Beloved Community is still the dream in God's heart for His world. It is the community His Son will establish fully.

Americans today really have no clue how fortunate they are that the social revolution of Civil Rights came through followers of Jesus. Their commitment to courageous, non-violent, change rooted in biblical values is the moral capital that every American is enjoying today. What shifted the conscience of our nation in the 1960's was hundreds of years of prayer in little shacks, back woods, and cotton fields. Those songs and prayers were heard and collected in heavenly bowls. They got tipped in the 1950's and the voice of a prophet, like Martin King, Jr, was heard again in the land. Sooner or later, prayer changes the world.

It would have been a very different and much more violent movement for change had the voice of Malcolm X, the eloquent, charismatic preacher of the Nation of Islam, been the one that prevailed. There were plenty of reasons why Black Americans could have turned to violence to liberate themselves from a spiritually deaf, oppressing White society. But it was Black Maids walking to White houses in Montgomery during the day and then walking to Black houses of worship in Montgomery at night that saved America from itself.

I had known a bit about my Uncle Bob's friendship with Martin King, but it wasn't until I visited him in 1999 in his home in Seattle that I got him to talk about their early days. He remembered when Martin and a few others were meeting the morning after a large White Citizens Council rally in Montgomery. At that gathering there was a dramatic entry by Police Commissioner Clyde Sellers who came in shouting. "Hold on! I'm coming! I'm with you! I'm with you!" It had the effect of completely polarizing Montgomery down racial lines and the year long siege by the White community to resist the demands of the Black community over desegregating city buses set in.

The members of the Alabama Council on Human Relations were saddened over the events of the night before. Bob's eyes moistened as he remembered Martin saying with conviction, "As long as I am a minister of the Gospel of Jesus Christ I have to believe in the possibility of human change." Martin would trust Bob to preach two or three times at Dexter Avenue Baptist Church during the bus boycott while he was rallying financial support around the country to keep the protest going.

When Lucy and I moved to Birmingham in 1998 and became a part of Sardis Missionary Baptist Church our pastor, Rev. Samuel Pettagrue, Jr., became a dear leader and friend. Sam grew up in Atlanta in Ralph Abernathy's church. He was mentored into the role of Baptist preacher by Dr. Abernathy, who was one of Martin's best friends. Sam would move to Birmingham to take the pulpit at Sardis.

I experienced a fatherly love and mentoring from Sam that marked me. His spiritual authority is what covered me as I ministered on Black Colleges and built friendships deep within the African-American community. Before his retirement, Sam had gained city-wide influence. His friendship with a white pastor, Frank Barker of Briarwood Presbyterian, was a source of years of transformational leadership in the church of Birmingham across deep racial divides.

Staying in partnership with strong African-American leadership keeps me connected to the spirit of Dr. King's dream for the Beloved Community today. Dr. Martin Luther King, Jr.'s spirit is still marching.

Alex Anderson

Alex and Felicia Anderson have five kids. Since Alex died suddenly in early January of 2002 at the age of 47, Felicia has continued to raise the family while carrying on the campus ministry of her husband at the Atlanta University Center's Historically Black Colleges.

Alex died two days before he was to be the first morning speaker for the InterVarsity National Staff Conference. His death was sobering to the 1200 staff gathered. The timing of his passing was God's way of highlighting the quality and character of Alex's life of faith to our whole spiritual family. Many of us wondered how Alex's massive legacy as an apostle to a generation of college students could be carried forward.

Alex was a dynamic man of prayer. As the National Director of InterVarsity's Black Campus Ministries, he mentored many campus staff, but he never stopped getting into whatever old vehicle God had provided to hit the road to see students and their families. He loved all students, but Alex had a calling to reach Black students and he especially had a heart for Historically Black Colleges.

In 2002, out of my concern that Alex's ministry to Black Colleges continue, I made a map of all 105 Historically Black Colleges in America. As I prayed for them it became my ambition, with God's help, to physically visit and pray on site for every official Historically Black College and University campus from Pennsylvannia to Texas. On November 9, 2009, I finished the journey at Huston-Tillotson

College in Austin. It would take another book to chronicle the prayers, encounters, conversations, and revelations of the Black College prayer walk. But one thing I never failed to do at each school was ask God to answer every prayer that Alex ever prayed for Black students and Black campuses in America.

Perhaps the call of God to carry Alex' burden for Black students and Black colleges came to me because of another special act of Jubilee worship in 1991. I was directing a college student conference around the theme of Jesus, Justice, and Jubilee. As I studied the Year of Jubilee in Leviticus 25 and learned about God's design to restore inheritances, forgive debts, and give the land and its people rest every 50 years, a thought began to grow. God began to speak to me about a table I had inherited from Gabriel Hughes. One of his slaves had made this table during a period before the Civil War. Lucy and I considered ourselves fortunate to have inherited one of the oldest artifacts in the Hughes family.

I remember turning to Lucy one night in bed and asking her to consider that we give the table to Alex and Felicia and their family as an act of Jubilee worship at the end of the conference. She was rather bothered at the idea at first. 'I would rather give away my wedding ring than that family heirloom." I understood her feeling. It was irreplaceable. But she went along with the idea enough to put the table under a blanket in the back of our car as we drove to the conference.

On the last day, I assured Lucy that I was not forcing her to give it away. I remember her quiet tears as we carried the table from the car to the main gathering room. She wimpered, "This is my Isaac." As Abraham was asked to sacrifice his son Isaac, this was the most precious thing she had ever been asked to offer to the Lord.

As I closed the conference, I asked our sons to come up along with Alex and his family. I explained the origin of the little table before us all. I explained how in the spirit of Jesus, justice, and Jubilee we as descendents of former slave owners wanted to honor God and give the table to the descendents of former slaves. One of the women there said she felt that the prayers of the slave who made the table were answered that day.

Seven years later, our family moved from Florida to Shelby County, Alabama. I began to pioneer a student fellowship at the local black college. Alex would drive over from Atlanta to supervise me as a White man serving Black students at Miles College. At my kitchen table he told me how his grandfather had also lived in Shelby County. Like my Dad, it was the last place he lived in Alabama. But Alex's granddad was fleeing a lynch mob and moved to Kansas where Alex would later be born before moving to California. It felt good for us to be back in Shelby County, around a new table in a new generation.

It was such a shock to learn in 2002 that Alex had suddenly passed. He died before so many of the dreams he had were fulfilled.

When a saint dies, they and their prayers are still alive in Heaven. We can pray to God *with* the saints by agreeing with their prayers. We will join them one day. Until then, may the crowd of witnesses on Earth walk in agreement with the cloud of witnesses in Heaven for all that is in the heart of our King!

Chapter 16

The Nature of Faith

"The only thing that counts is faith working through love."
(Gal.5:6)

What is Faith?

If the Cloud of Witnesses in Heaven are those who have finished their marathon of faith well, we should take a closer look at the 66 Books' way of defining faith.

Hebrews chapter eleven begins with a great working definition.

Now faith is being certain of what we hope for and the substance of what we do not see. This is what the ancients were commended for. ...And without faith, it is impossible to please God, because anyone who comes to Him must believe that He exists and that He rewards those who earnestly seek Him. (Heb 11:1,6)

Certainty and Substance

We do not typically think of invisible future things as certain or substantial. Our cultural world view places certainty and substance on what is material now. We Westerners have been grazing for centuries on a rationalistic, materialistic worldview called "Modernity". Followers of Jesus are affected by this worldview in the same way that fish swimming in a polluted lake are affected by the toxins in the water.

Not everything about the worldview of Modernity is bad or wrong, it just isn't taking the unseen world as seriously as God. This thinking is underneath the false premise of dichotomies like "sacred and secular" or "faith and science" as two different things that don't mix in real life.

Much of the less technologically advanced world lives with a visceral awareness of unseen realities. Without a revelation of God, this tends to bend in to the fear side of our human nature. Cultures all over the world throughout time have worshipped whatever concept of the spirit world they can come up with based on available information. Because we were made for relationship with a God that we currently do not see, our souls are inevitably prone to worship the highest concept we can construct until we discover the real thing.

In our materialistic, scientific world, atheists exercise "faith" in the unknown by their doctrine of origins. The old PBS show "Cosmos" hosted by the late Dr. Carl Sagan, began with, "The cosmos is all there was, all there is, and all there will be." Scientist Stephen Hawking is a popular voice for the material world view today. This theory can be stated with bravado, but ironically cannot be proven scientifically, because if humans are more than chemicals, Carl Sagan is wrong. So the question remains. Are there non-material realities present in the universe we all share?

Fear is a substance, but you can't measure it in a test tube. You cannot see it with your eyes in one sense, but you can observe it spread from person to person. Love, or our concept of love, is invisible in one sense, but it is very strongly felt. The impact of its presence is profound in its ability to change an environment or a human heart.

In his book, *Created for Influence,* author Will Ford notes that "influence" was defined by the ancients as "that ethereal fluid or *substance* that flows from the stars and affects human behavior." We get words like "influenza" from this concept. The "flu" was invisible to the unaided eye, but it was highly contagious and its effects were clearly felt and seen.

If fear and love are invisible substances that we can easily comprehend on a practical level, then what about *faith*? Is it a substance from Heaven as the Bible claims? Does it flow not just from "the stars," but from the Maker of the stars?

Psalm 147 says, "*He determines the number of the stars and calls them each by name.*"

Psalm 148 says, "*Praise the Lord from the heavens, praise Him in the heights above. Praise Him all His angels, praise Him all His heavenly inhabitants. Praise Him, sun and moon, praise Him you shining stars. Praise Him you highest heavens and you waters above the skies. Let them praise the Name of the Lord for He commanded and they were created. He set them in place forever and ever; He gave a decree that will never pass away. ...Let everyone praise the Name of the Lord, for His name alone is highest, for His splendor is above the earth and the heavens.*"

Richard Dawkins, another popular atheist speaker says, "Why pay attention to the writings of ancient Middle Eastern goat herders?" He reduces the literary and historic phenomenon of an ancient monotheistic witness over thousands of years to a mocking one liner and MANY in our culture are buying it. I say if you look at the beauty and miracle of creation and humanity itself, it takes more faith NOT to believe that a wise, loving God was not behind it all.

No-name Israelites from thousands of years ago sang the praises of an eternal God and set an example for all the rest of us to follow. Their praise songs are a part of the worship chorus that never stops in the Cloud of Witnesses. The faith substance of every generation of saints is the influence we inherit when we place our faith in the One God of Heaven and Earth.

The Anchor for our Faith

Jesus said, "The work of God is this: to believe in the One He has sent." (John 6:29)

The *object* of our faith is what is critical. God-pleasing faith is rooted in trusting the real Jesus - a real Man on a real Throne in a real Heaven coming back in real time to your neighborhood. It isn't enough to have faith in faith, or hope in hope. It isn't enough to plant your "seed of faith" to your favorite television ministry to get the material or spiritual results of what they apparently have. What God requires is faith and hope chained to the Person of Jesus. No man-made object or belief system will suffice.

The writer of Hebrews says, "We have this hope as an anchor for the soul, firm and secure. It enters the Most Holy Place in the Temple, behind the curtain, where Jesus, who went before us, has entered on our behalf." (6:19-20)

Imagine your soul has an anchor. Have you been to an ocean dock and seen the kind of chains used to hoist the anchors of large ships? Each link in the chain is HUGE. Now imagine your soul is anchored with this massive chain, not to the bottom of the sea, but up to a Man in Heaven beyond the merely physical world. Nothing in the universe can break the chain that binds you to Him. Jesus is your Anchor behind the Veil of the sky.

Christians, like anyone, are vulnerable to a materialistic world view. In Scripture a whole army appeared on the doorstep of Elisha at his home in Dothan. Elisha could see the Lord of the Angel armies and was unshaken by the number of men and spears in front of him. He asked God to open the eyes of his quaking servant to see the reality of Heaven. Then the servant knew what Elisha knew. "Many more are those who are for us, than those who are against us." (2 Kings 6:16)

We need the eyeglasses of true faith today as much as the little servant in Dothan. To have faith is more than having a right understanding. *It is having a right spirit.*

Three Things Remain – Faith, Hope, and Love

Any astronomer can tell you that our sun is dying. If we are still here on earth in a few billion years, it will not be a good day. But even as the sun goes through death throes, its matter will continue in some form.

The Bible claims this universe that seems so lasting to us can be remade into a new one whenever the Creator pleases. In fact, the Bible agrees with Einstein that all matter is actually negotiable. (E=MC2) energy {E} is equal to Matter {M} times the Speed of Light {C} squared.) But Scripture goes further and states that what is MORE certain are invisible or spiritual realities. The quark is the smallest sub atomic particle ever observed during atom smashing experiments. The quark is essentially light energy and vibration. It is woven into the fabric of our universe. I believe the quark is an echo of God's voice. When God spoke creation He said, "Let there be light." The vibration and light of God's voice is sustaining the universe at all times.

According to the Bible, our universe is the expression of the very person of God through Jesus His Son.

The Son is the radiance of God's glory and the exact represen-tation of his being, sustaining all things by his powerful word. (Hebrews 1:3)

Jesus as the God-Man and Living Word is also the Creator of all things.

He is the image of the invisible God, the firstborn over all creation. For by Him all things were created that are in heaven and that are on earth, visible and invisible, whether thrones or dominions or principalities or powers. All things were created through Him and for Him. And He is before all things, and in Him all things consist. (Colossians 1:15-17)

The world view of the Bible is plain. Our world is more than matter. Matter matters. But spiritual reality matters most. God is supreme. "*And now abide faith, hope, love, these three; but the greatest of these is love.*" (1 Corinthians 13:13) Faith, hope, and love are spiritual realities that have their existence in God Himself.

Tim Keller is a pastor in New York City. He says that our common use of the word "hope" and the Biblical use of the word "hope" are very different ideas. We say things like, "I hope it doesn't

rain, today." or "I hope I have made the right choice to get married."
Our use of the word communicates a measure of uncertainty about
the outcome. It is basically wishful thinking.

Not so with biblical hope. Paul says, that after everything is said
and done, there are three things that still stand: faith, hope, and love.
Biblical hope is not optimism, it is realism. It is a hope unseen, but
rooted in the really real. The Christian confession is not "I hope
Jesus is Lord." It is "Jesus is Lord! My hope is in Him!"

Biblical hope does not deny suffering. Jesus' example affirms
it as part of the birth pains of a greater Age to come. Biblical hope
doesn't fail when calamity comes. Calamities will always come in
this Age. But God is good and fully in control. Only the faith of the
Bible offers a relationship with the God of history who has made us
all and died to restore us after our rejection of Him.

Jesus is the Author and Finisher of our Faith, our Anchor of
Hope beyond the Veil, the Lover of our Souls. Because of the bodily
resurrection of Jesus, our hope is certain. He is invisible now, yes,
but certain to anyone who knows Him by faith. Certainty comes not
by an ability to conjure up positive feelings, but because of daily
choices to trust God as Father. We bank on the integrity of His promises to us in Jesus. The gift of His Spirit is a down payment on what
is to come. Our Father God has given us His Son *and* His Spirit to
confirm His intentions!

Real Faith Goes Beyond Our Lifespan

Adam and Eve, and the generations before Noah, lived close to a
thousand years. After Noah, the lifespan for our race was set by God
at 120 years. Moses prayed a prayer written as Psalm 90 that says,
"The years of our life are seventy; eighty if we are strong."

We have a life expectancy of 70 to 80 years in America and then
you meet Jesus. Every human being has a certain measure of days
to get ready to stand before Jesus and hear what He has to say about
us. If you live in an unjust nation, like Zimbabwe, your life expectancy is a lot shorter. All flesh is like grass. None of us is promised
tomorrow, but we are promised eternity!

This life can seem so "permanent." Facing our physical death is very intimidating, so we avoid the topic if we can. But Jesus gives his followers SO much reason to have biblical hope beyond our physical death. Listen to what Martha's friend told her before commanding Lazarus to come out of a four day old stinking tomb:

"I am the Resurrection and the Life, He who believes in me will live, even though he dies. Whoever lives and believes in Me will never die. Do you believe this, (Martha)?

'Yes, Lord,' she told Him, 'I believe that you are the Messiah, the Son of God, who was to come into the world.'" (John 11:25-27)

Martha had faith in the word of Jesus and she got her brother back for a little while longer. But Martha died. And Lazarus did, again. Even miracles of resurrection and political revolutions for justice are temporary tokens of a greater Age to come. They, like the Cloud of Witnesses, inspire us to greater faith in the times still in front of us.

A Recent Addition to the Cloud of Witnesses

While writing this chapter, Lucy was attending the funeral of her cousin, Morris Shepard McCastlain, Jr. I had the privilege to lead Shep to Jesus more than 20 years ago. His conversion wasn't dramatic in the sense that he had lots of obvious sin to repent of like me. He was always "moral" and a joy to everybody. I think Shep's faith walk with Jesus was deep because he never had the same life expectations most people have.

During childhood, Shep developed a brain tumor. Cobalt radiation treatments gave Shep forty-five pretty good years. In the end it was the very same cobalt treatments that probably caused the brain tumor that ended his life.

Shep never married and never had a promising career. The tumor affected his pituitary gland causing him to look younger than others his age. He lived with a brave awareness of his limitations. But Shep overcame, with the help of Jesus, the bouts of bitterness anyone in his shoes would face. He was one of the most positive people I have ever known. He was intelligent and compassionate to the very end.

As Lucy and I were visiting him for the last time a few days before he died, we read this passage to Shep from Paul's second letter to the church at Corinth, chapter five. Read it as if you were in that room with us by Shep's bed in his last hours on earth.

Now we know that if the earthly tent we live in is destroyed, we have a building from God, an eternal house in Heaven, not built by human hands. Meanwhile we groan, longing to be clothed with our Heavenly dwelling because when we are clothed, we will not be found naked. For while we are in this tent, we groan and are burdened, because we do not wish to be unclothed but to be clothed with our heavenly dwelling, so that what is mortal may be swallowed up by life. Now it is God who has made us for this purpose and has given us the Spirit as a deposit, guaranteeing what is to come.

Therefore we are always confident and know that as long as we are at home in the body we are away from the Lord. We live by faith, not by sight. We are confident, I say, and would prefer to be away from the body and at home with the Lord. So we make it our goal to please Him, whether we are at home in the body or away from it. For we must all appear before the judgment seat of Christ, that each one may receive what is due him for the things done while in the body, whether good or bad.

Lucy looked deeply into her cousin's eyes and wept as she told Shep how much he pleased the Lord. Then I heard him say these words. They are the last clear words I heard him speak.

"I have *so* much to look forward to."

Our Turn

A life of growing faith in Jesus is what pleases God. He is trustworthy and Jesus enjoys the process of helping our fearful, blind hearts as we learn to trust Him fully. God is so much more than what any of us know. Only maturing trust will help us experience more of who He is. It will take eternity and people from every language and nation throughout time to *begin* to reflect His glory!

Beware of faith solely defined as what produces spectacular results in the realm of health, wealth, and social prosperity. Powerful healings and open doors of provision are wonderful blessings from God! But, God exists for more than meeting our culturally felt needs in this present Age. Miraculous breakthroughs are tokens of eternal things to come and are not automatic signs of God's pleasure with us. Receiving a divine healing or miracle of any kind does not exempt us from living a daily life of faith and obedience.

Faith is a growing trust in the leadership of Jesus. Great faith is a long obedience through great trials. Faith is not for us to get what we desire from God, but for God to get what He desires in us.

Biblical faith is about trusting God to meet our *real* needs. Paul promised that "everyone who wants to live a godly life in Christ Jesus will be persecuted." (2 Tim. 3:12) I do not have a felt need to be persecuted! But suffering patiently for God's purposes is one of the greatest gifts God can give us, because it produces maturity in a way that prosperity alone cannot. The Cloud of Witnesses in Hebrews 11 and people from our own experience provide examples for how we too can keep our eyes steady on the God who holds the future.

Our lives are a relay race. We connect to the forerunners of faith before us as we redeem our own time. Jesus is our chief Forerunner. He is looking to pass the baton of His Spirit to a new generation who will run their race of faith. Are you in? Good! It is our turn.

Finishing Life Well

Part Five

Living the Culture of the Kingdom

Chapter 17

The Sermon on the Mount Value System

"Now when he saw the crowds, he went up on a mountainside and sat down. His disciples came to him, and he began to teach them saying: 'Blessed are the poor in spirit, for theirs is the kingdom of heaven.'" (Matthew 5:1-3)

Praying For the Enemy

Years ago, a poll was taken of non-religious people to see which of all the sayings of Jesus from the Bible they could recall.

At the top of the list was a line from Jesus' Sermon on the Mount recorded in Matthew's Gospel chapters five, six, and seven. It was three words. "Love your enemies."

I find it interesting that the thing non-believers remember most is what believers remember least!

Jesus completely redefines what love looks like in His teaching of how He wants His Kingdom subjects to live. Let's look at the broader statement He made.

You have heard that it was said, 'An eye for an eye and a tooth for a tooth.' But I say to you, do not resist one who is evil. If anyone strikes you on the right cheek, turn to him the other also. And if anyone would sue you and take your coat, let him have your cloak as well. If anyone forces you to go one mile, go with him two miles.

Give to him who begs from you and do not refuse him who would borrow from you.

You have heard that it was said, 'You shall love your neighbor and hate your enemy.' But I say to you, love your enemies and pray for those who persecute you so that you may be sons of your Father who is in Heaven. For He makes the sun rise on the evil and on the good, and sends rain on the just and the unjust. For if you love those who love you, what reward have you? Do not even the tax collectors do the same? And if you salute only your brethren, what more are you doing than others? Do not even the Gentiles do the same? You, therefore, must be perfect, as your heavenly Father is perfect. (Matthew 5:38-48)

Transcending Culture

The Sermon on the Mount in Matthew chapters five, six, and seven encapsulate the core values of Jesus' heart and message. It is the value system of Christ's Kingdom. Living these values always produce revolutionary, transformational cultures. The Kingdom of God is the most subversive of all forces led by the most subversive of all leaders. The culture of humility, mercy, and truth in radical 24/7 union with Jesus through prayer in community is the salt and light of eternity preserving and enlightening our dark and dying world.

We can't dumb down the Sermon on the Mount. We have to take it on its own terms and let it rock our own ideas about how life works. Living it means entering a culture of humility, repentance, purity, generosity, servant-hood, persecution, and maximum adventure. More than any text in the Bible, it is the key to doing and finishing life well. The late theologian John R. Stott called it the "Kingdom counter-culture."

Can its radical principles be applied in our Western Postmodern culture of pleasure and convenience? Oh yeah. Why? Because the values of the Sermon on the Mount transcend fallen human nature itself! The life of Jesus uproots everything dead inside of each one of us. The Kingdom of God is supra-cultural. Jesus can't be put in

a box. He is Lord of All. He transcends all cultures, religious struc-
tures, movements, philosophies, and story lines.

Descending into Greatness

The message of the Sermon on the Mount is that the lower we
go in this life, the higher we go in the next. Are there rewards in this
life? Yes. But the cool thing about the blessings of Jesus is that they
don't stop when we do.

The teachings of Jesus require militant humility and radical self-
giving. This life can only grow in the soil of relentless dialog with
Him as a real Man in Heaven dwelling by His Spirit in our hearts. It
also takes a *community* of similarly weak people stumbling forward
together to sustain a Sermon on the Mount lifestyle. But even those
communities can never be successfully institutionalized or patented.
Ministry models don't die for you. Organizations and political states
can't turn the other cheek. Only people can. Institutions have a
vested interest to protect, punish, and provide. Institutions, though
they seem so much more powerful, are actually weaker than one
humble heart when it comes to real sacrifice.

Dr. Martin Luther King, Jr. observed that groups of people tend
toward moral weakness, not moral strength. When we get together,
our collective wimpiness wants to hide behind the skirts of compromise rather than die for ideals and principles. Only the most courageous and pure of leaders can stand up to their own people and
contend for the values in God's heart. Jesus settled the issue about
the kind of community He was living for, by dying for it. His death
wasn't so we wouldn't have to suffer like He did. His life of humility
was intended to show us *how* to do the same.

It can get confusing when the leaders of our church institutions
live more like the Jesus who is sitting on the Throne of Heaven, than
the Jesus who promised we would have tribulation and persecution
in this life. Jesus said, "Greater love has no one than this: to lay
down one's life for one's friend." (John 15:3) Jesus did that for His
enemies, too.

So as much as I enjoy being the president of a ministry organization, that is not the litmus test of my life in Christ. My life is

hidden with Christ in God. My life is more than who I am when I am holding a microphone. How I act when I have nothing to gain lets me know if I am really representing Jesus in the earth. True leaders embody the vision and values of the community they are charged to shepherd. The true shepherd lays down his life for the sheep.

Embodying the Community of the King

I am not knocking institutional leadership. It is a servant role involving great humility, wisdom, Christ-like character, and costly organizational authority. But whether we are a Pope or President in this life, doesn't mean that is the job we will have in the Kingdom Jesus will set up. When Jesus said that the meek will inherit the Earth, He was not being rhetorical. The most humble, merciful, loyal, persevering and truthful people are going to be the ones with proximity to Jesus in the Age to come.

The fact that greatness in the culture of the Kingdom is so rooted in the hidden responses of the human heart means that only God sees what is really going on in there! God will choose those who loved Jesus the most and knew Him best to serve nearest His table in eternity. It doesn't matter what your job title is now. The poor in spirit, whom Jesus promised would see God, includes a forgotten girl in South Sudan who trembles at His presence. The hearts of every person on the planet are open books to our Father.

That is why Jesus makes the whole sermon so *personal*. It truly is about a dynamic love relationship with Him that really counts for eternity. It doesn't matter what people think about us. They don't get a vote at the judgment seat. At the beginning of the Sermon on the Mount Jesus says we are to consider ourselves blessed when we are suffering because of Him. At the end of the sermon our whole future is based on whether we listened to Him and did what He said. If Jesus isn't the Messiah, He has a major ego problem!

No wonder we all try to rationalize and theologize this sermon away. It is completely at odds with the way we are tutored to get ahead in life. It is an upside down Kingdom where the elite are the marginalized, and the last in this world get to be first in the one coming.

The call of Jesus in the Sermon on the Mount was to "be perfect," like our Father in Heaven. That is a heavy word! In Luke's gospel, Jesus uses "merciful" as the ideal describing God's perfect Father Heart. "But love your enemies, do good to them and lend without expecting to get anything back. Then your reward will be great, and you will be sons of the Most High, because He is kind to the ungrateful and wicked. Be merciful, just as your Father is merciful." (Luke 6:35-36)

Chapter 18

A Perfect Heart

"The LORD is compassionate and gracious, slow to anger, abounding in love." (Psalm 103:8)

The Goal of Mercy

Following the trail of our Father's mercy leads us to encountering His perfect heart like David did. Our Father delights to show us mercy, because what He really wants is relationship. His goal is intimacy, not mere pardon.

If you killed my son, in a culture that gives me the right to kill you, you probably wouldn't want to come around my house. If I renounce my right to kill you, you might appreciate getting off the hook. You might even want to initiate personal contact.

Knowing that I won't kill you is probably an important step in beginning a relationship with me! It opens the door. But there is still a relationship to be grown and that requires a dynamic process that can't be rushed or manufactured.

What if you knew that my main reason for forgiving you was so that I could get to know you and we could become *friends*? How would that impact your desire to reciprocate? It would require some uncomfortable humility on your part to receive that measure of mercy, wouldn't it? It would probably help our friendship if I never reminded you of how deeply you wounded my heart. Frankly, it wouldn't do any good anyway. It wouldn't bring my son back and it would probably just make me feel angry and you feel guilty.

It is a bit like that with God after accepting His mercy. He didn't send Jesus to die for us just for kicks. The Cross opens the door to what God really wants. He desires a dynamic and intimate relationship with you now and partnership in the Age to come. A deeper relationship is the goal of His mercy! It is what brings Him the most joy! Let the thousand foot tsunami of His mercy really hit you as you gaze at that naked Man on a bloody stick. This isn't tit-for-tat. God doesn't *have* to love you. He loves you because He *longs* to.

To return to my analogy, if you kill my son, I forgive you for it, and you *still* have no sorrow or desire for relationship, then you have a big problem with God. "'Vengeance is mine, I will repay.' says the Lord." It is far better for enemies to become friends, but either way God will bring about justice. Blood will always be answered with blood. The blood of Jesus that covers our sin speaks the better word of mercy.

Unconditional and Conditional Grace

The great gift of God to anyone who asks for it is the perfect life of Jesus *given* to us at the Cross. God plants Himself right inside our hearts when we open the door to Him in faith. Jesus' indestructible life works from our insides out to *keep* us growing in that ever-flowing *gift* of righteousness in real time.

Author John Piper, in his book *Future Grace*, writes that there is a difference between unconditional grace and conditional grace. Unconditional grace is God rescuing us apart from any effort or merit of our own. Conditional grace is based on our willful response, positively or negatively, to God's help every day. As we abide in His love, mercy, and truth, choosing His will over our own, we dynamically mature into people who more and more reflect the character of Jesus. By God's grace, we do life *and* finish life well!

God's help is available 24/7. He showers His goodness on the "just and the unjust". The fact that He took care of the universe last night while you and I slept is a part of the unconditional grace of God in our lives. But there are also "if/then" commands in the Bible.

These are the conditional promises of grace from God. He promises help based on our obedience. It is how He conforms our lives to His.

Conditional grace is free, but it helps to *ask* for it. Gods' mercy is new every morning, but don't take it for granted. Acknowledging Him as a Good Dad, thanking Him for waking us up, and receiving His love as if it was the first and last day of our lives is the starting point of living in His Kingdom. We enter the Kingdom with nothing. We are most human when we are in touch with our "poverty" of spirit and utter dependence on God.

The Book of James, written by Jesus' half brother, mirrors in practical ways the values of the Sermon on the Mount. James 4:10, "Humble yourselves before the Lord and He will lift you up" is a re-statement of "Blessed are the poor in spirit, for theirs is the Kingdom." There is an implied if/then command here. IF we humble ourselves before God, THEN He will lift us up.

Humbling ourselves is not a means to an end. God doesn't owe us anything. Since God knows what we need and who He is making us to become, we aren't guaranteed the raise, or recognition, or miracle we want. Circumstances may get *worse* for us. Then we have another opportunity to believe our Good Father has something better than what we asked for!

What we *are* promised when we choose humility is more intimacy with God. He *will* lift us up, but it will be on His terms and timetable. The question we must ask is, "Am I okay with that?" Our answer will depend on how much we value Him and His way of doing life. Jesus' value system clashed with His generation.

"Whoever can be trusted with very little can also be trusted with much, and whoever is dishonest with very little will also be dishonest with much. So if you have not been trustworthy in handling worldly wealth, who will trust you with true riches? And if you have not been trustworthy with someone else's property, who will give you property of your own?

"No servant can serve two masters. Either he will hate the one and love the other, or he will be devoted to the one and despise the other. You cannot serve both God and Money."

*The Pharisees, who loved money, heard all this and were sneering at Jesus. He said to them, "You are the ones who justify yourselves in the eyes of men, but God knows your hearts. **What is highly valued among men is detestable in God's sight."** (Luke 16:10-15)*

Going as low in humility as we know before the majesty of God is the key to gaining a more real encounter with Him, which leads to more humility, which leads to more encounter, which leads to more humility, which leads to...

The Grace of Mercy

Mercy and forgiveness from God is unconditional at the cross of Jesus Christ. We can't resist His saving grace any more than running from lightning. Bam! But after we are awakened to life in God by grace through faith, God gives us conditional promises to live out like: "Blessed are the merciful, for they will be shown mercy." (Matthew 5:7)

In Matthew 6:15, the conditional result of not showing mercy is terrifyingly clear. "If you do not forgive others, God will not forgive you." Forgiveness is "love your enemies" in action. That's what God does for us and, if we are His kids, we do it for others. Perhaps the greatest test of a follower of Jesus is our willingness to give and receive genuine mercy.

Jesus corrected a ministry leader by the example of a woman who had just washed His feet with her tears. Anyone in that room would have rather been the proud host at the head of the table instead of the disheveled woman beneath it. Jesus said, "Those who have been forgiven much, love much." This broken-hearted, grateful woman was in touch with her desperate need for mercy. She humbled herself before Jesus and He raised her up.

Humility isn't groveling. God wants us to hate our sin, but God does not want anyone to hate themselves. We are in a love relationship with Him based on infinite mercy that won't change throughout eternity.

When we pray for and forgive those who have intentionally or unintentionally offended us we are not denying hard facts. God doesn't deny anything that is "true". He knows the event *and* its reverberating pain. When the Bible says that God casts all our sins into a sea of forgetfulness, it doesn't mean He is some kind of "Pollyanna" who pulls the wool over His own eyes because He can't handle the ugly reality in front of Him. God CHOOSES to cover our sin with the blood of Jesus so He can relate to us as if we had never offended Him in any way. That is GREAT mercy! Great mercy produces the rarest substance in the universe — perfect love.

Learning Humility

The unconditional grace of the Cross of Jesus moves us from condemnation to pardon. Conditional grace moves us from pardon to partnership with Jesus. Followers of Jesus don't sweat whether or not we will be in eternity. But real Jesus lovers *do sweat* in the process of maturing through faith, obedience, and enduring discipline as God's kids. Humility is Christianity 101, 201, 301, and... You don't graduate from this class until you finish your race.

For it was fitting that He, for whom and by whom all things exist, in bringing many sons to glory, should make the forerunner of their salvation perfect through suffering... For because He Himself has suffered and been tempted, He is able to help those who are tempted. (Hebrews 2:10, 18)

We need to learn from the humility of Jesus. He told us to.

"Come to me all you who are weary and burdened, and I will give you rest. Take my yoke upon you and learn from me, for I am gentle and humble in heart, and you will find rest for your souls." (Matthew 11:28-29)

Jesus went through a process of learning humility in His life. Humility is a choice to go lower in service, rather than to assert ones power or rights. Jesus and Moses are the only two in the Bible described as humble. Moses had only one moment of stepping out of humility and it cost him entrance into the Promised Land. Jesus *passed* His heart test in the Garden of Gethsemane and finished well hanging from the tree.

Only the most powerful people can be the most humble, because the greatness of humility rests in the degree of the choice to descend. Jesus, as the God-Man is the most powerful and the most humble One of all. "Though He was rich, yet for your sakes He became poor, so that you through His poverty might become rich." (2 Cor. 8:9)

Jesus walked the road before us so He can help us travel it by His Spirit living in us. His promise to never leave us is really good because this "love your enemies" thing sounds ridiculous! Maybe that is why non-Christians remember it and why they aren't Christians! Let's not forget these words of Jesus. They may be the most important ones to, well ... *do*; especially, if those who love their enemies and pray for them are the ones who most resemble the perfect heart of their Father.

Chapter 19

Saved By a Holy Fool

"What does the Lord require of you, but to do justly, love mercy, and walk humbly with your God?" (Micah 6:8)

Alternate Ending

On DVD's there are sometimes special features that include alternate endings by the director. Here is my version of a possible alternate ending in the Garden of Gethsemane just before Jesus is betrayed, arrested, and taken to trial.

My scene opens with Jesus pleading with His three closest friends to stay awake and keep Him company while He is on the verge of panic thinking about what is going to happen to Him over the next twenty-four hours or so. Peter, James, and John promise Him they are with Him "all the way" and that they "have His back," yada, yada, yada.

Jesus goes back to pleading with His Dad to reconsider the costly plan to save the world. Satan is licking his chops in the shadows. Jesus goes back to "Rocky and the Thunder Brothers" to be encouraged. Three times. Each time He finds His friends sound asleep instead of praying. On the third time He looks up to His Father in Heaven disgustedly and says, "That's it! I'm done. These guys can't even stay awake and pray for me *one* hour. After all the things I have done for them."

Then He lays into his "best buddies" one by one. "James and John, I know you guys are just after the power and offices I can give you when I get inaugurated. Wasn't it just a few days ago that you came with your *Mommy* to ask me to let you sit next to me in My throne room? I overheard the whispers around supper tonight with you guys jockeying for position. You *said* you could drink from the same cup of suffering that I have to drink from. Well, I'm drinkin' it and you ain't! So you can just forget about all your political ambitions."

"And you 'Mister Solid-as-a-Rock.' Didn't I just finish telling you that you would deny Me three times before the sun comes up. Satan and I just had a conversation and I went to bat for you. He said he wanted to get you alone and see what you are made of. I told him to buzz off. But you know what? He is sitting right over there trying to interrupt My conversation with Dad and I think I'll just let him have you after all."

"What's the point?! How am I supposed to die for a world of people who hate my guts and you guys can't even be there for me the one time I really need you!? Well, they can just all go to Hell and so can you!"

Scene ends.

Jesus Practices What He Preaches

Thank God Jesus was nothing like the one in my alternate ending! Jesus did not forsake His destiny. He resisted that temptation to the point of sweating blood as He cried out to His Father. Rather than becoming bitter toward us, He drank the bitter cup for us.

Sometimes the road to loving our enemies begins by praying for our closest friends when they have deeply disappointed us. Judas did become Jesus' enemy that night, but Jesus didn't stop loving him. Gaining mastery over our emotions toward others is what allows us to do the really hard work of loving people "in spite of" who they are or what they are doing. It is that agape kind of love again. It is "perfect" love. It is how our Dad loves us.

You see, I am one of those sleeping friends. I need to let the things that I do, or don't do, that "disappoint" Jesus drive me to

Him. Why? Because I *want* to stay awake for Him. I really do. I am *trying* to stay awake. God help me. My desire to stay awake is there, but my ability is pathetically weak. We are all weak. We are all rebels and losers. A line was drawn and we crossed it. A destiny was given and we lost it.

Unconditional love creates havoc in our hearts. When we can't find a selfish motive behind an action, we are stumped. It puts a rift in the time/space continuum of our psyche. Human beings aren't supposed to behave unselfishly. Jesus' love isn't based on a certain human response.

When Jesus, from the cross, forgave those crucifying Him, He had settled the issue in the garden the night before. He was not a victim. He willingly, even *joyfully*, gave His life for us while we were in the depth of our dark condition. Jesus said, "Even the Son of Man came not to be served, but to serve, and to give His life as a ransom for many." (Mark 10:45)

His choice to go through the crushing of His life was His greatest act of TRUST in the leadership of His Father. Did love for us keep Jesus on the cross? Yes. But far beyond that, love for His Father helped him accept His life as a guilt offering for our sin and to raise Him up after His death. It was the plan announced through the prophet Isaiah hundreds of years before.

"Yet it was the *Lord's* will to crush him and *cause* him to suffer, and though the Lord makes his life a guilt offering, he will see his offspring and prolong his days." (Is 53:10)

In chapter two, I talked about the role of fear and desire and how our greatest fears and desires define who we become? Think about Jesus in the Garden. What was He most afraid of? Was it the rejection of men? He had already been rejected many times at this point. He even foretold Judas of his betrayal and Peter of his denial over dinner *that night*. Was it the pain of Jewish and Roman torture? That had to have been intimidating. But physical pain is temporary. Many have endured horrible physical torture throughout history.

Jesus looked squarely into His Father's zeal against sin and death and chose to receive the full penalty that was to fall on Him as the sin-bearer of the world. What Isaac feared his father Abraham would do to him on the altar of Moriah's hill thousands of years before, Jesus knew His Father was going through with. This time no angel would stay the hand of the Father. This time the Beloved Son would be crushed by His Dad. The cup Jesus begged three times for His Father to let pass was the bitter cup of God's zeal to destroy the curse of human sin and death by smashing His Son.

Jesus' prayer of submission to His Father's plan in Luke 22:5, "Nevertheless, not my will, but Yours be done," is the most mature prayer ever prayed.

God Wants Mature Prayers

Many prayers are not answered because we are not asking for what is already the will and purpose of God for our lives. God wants us to ask for the most valuable things. The true riches of Heaven are His desires. Mature prayers start there. "God, make me who I need to be for You today." "Father, help me to serve Your purposes in the lives of those around me today." "Holy Spirit, give me the mind and heart of Jesus today." "Jesus, what are You thinking, what are You feeling, I ask to know?"

Eternity is based on God's desires, not ours. But a life of prayer causes those desires to become the same! The conversation of prayer we have with His heart is in order that we learn how to live well with Him in the Age to come. He wants us to imbibe His eternal value system. He wants to answer our prayers, but He is patiently waiting for the value system of our prayers to agree with His. Prayers that agree with His desires always get answered, sooner or later.

The Sermon on the Mount value of loving and praying for enemies is absurd if there is no Eternal Age. Jesus calls His followers to live upside down values in order to demonstrate to the world there is more to this life than this life. Jesus wants a Kingdom counter-culture until He returns.

A Love That Forgives is a Love that Suffers Long

To illustrate the subversive power of love to conquer all, I want to talk about Forrest Gump. Forrest Gump?! Bear with me! If you saw Tom Hanks play this character in the movie, you know that patiently suffering in love as Forrest did for his beloved, but wayward, Jenny is what leads to finishing life well. All of Jesus' followers are called to a life of faithful love that is usually invisible and often unimpressive, like Forrest Gump.

Forrest told us his Mama always said, "Stupid is as stupid does." Like sacrificing His Son on a terrible cross, God's wisdom often appears foolish. But a life of loving God and others is what proves wisest in the end. We can't love this way in our own strength. It takes the love of God to love God! It also takes the love of God to love others and ourselves. That doesn't bother our Father. He knows we can't live and love without Him. The answer is to let Him love us. That means we all qualify!

If what God requires for us to finish life well is also something God fully supplies, then He is absolutely just in all His ways. None of us will have an excuse when we stand before Jesus or see Him come from Heaven. Jesus will return and all will see He is the King of Kings and Lord of Lords. But what qualifies Him to lead us all is that He has already come with long suffering love as the Gump of Gumps.

"He had no beauty or majesty to attract us to him, nothing in his appearance that we should desire him. He was despised and rejected by men, a man of sorrows, and familiar with suffering. Like one from whom men hide their faces he was despised, and we esteemed him not."

If you have been broken by the relentless, extravagant love of Jesus, in the face of all your petty misuse of Him, you are on your way to discovering what Forrest Gump's Jenny found. We are saved by a Holy Fool who should have known when to give up on us long ago. But didn't.

Chapter 20

Becoming a
Forrest Gump Generation

"But God has chosen the foolish things of the world to put
to shame the wise, and God has chosen the weak things of
the world to put to shame the things that are mighty."
(1 Corinthians 1:27)

The Forrest Gump Anointing

"Anointing" is a term used in the Charismatic Christian community for a God-given characteristic. "Messiah" and "Christ" are Hebrew and Greek words respectively that both mean "Anointed One." Israel's kings and priests were anointed by the pouring of perfumed oil over their heads and bodies. They were to carry a fragrance that was pleasing to God and recognized by the people. The anointing was given distinctly for leadership among God's people. That is why Jesus was taunted, "If you are the Anointed One, come down from that cross." If Jesus could not save himself, how *could* He be the King of the Jews?

John the Baptizer anointed his cousin Jesus with the waters of the Jordan River. John came washing the humble in Israel with a baptism of repentance for the forgiveness of their sin. But Jesus had no sin. His baptism by John was in the tradition of Israel's kings being anointed by Israel's prophets. When John anointed Jesus it was to inaugurate a King, who was not only the Holy One of Israel, but the Lord of the Universe! His Kingdom had no political boundaries and no expiration date. A voice from Heaven said, "This is My Son, with whom I am well pleased!" John exclaimed, "Behold the Lamb of God who takes away the sin of the world!"

The anointing of Jesus as the Lamb of God was for sacrificial leadership. Before He ascended in authority to the Throne of God, Jesus descended in love to the depths of the grave. He became a fool in the eyes of men to demonstrate the wisdom of God. He was the original Forrest Gump! A Holy Fool who isn't stupid after all.

I like to think of my Uncle Bob as possessing a "Forrest Gump anointing." Let me explain what I mean. In the movie by the same name, Forrest Gump is a simpleton who has a knack for being on the scene when the doors of history are swinging. You might not notice him at the time, but when you replay the tape of historic moments, there is Forrest next to, say, Alabama Governor George Wallace as he stands in the "school house door" to block racial integration at the University of Alabama. Add to the fact that Forrest Gump went to the University of Alabama like my Uncle Bob before they both started changing the world and you have one of those movies- mirroring-our-lives deals.

The old Hughes home in Gadsden, Alabama is on Forrest Avenue. That is Forrest with two "R"'s because the street was named for Nathan Bedford Forrest the Confederate General who rode through town chasing Yankees during the Civil war. He later became the first Grand Wizard of the Ku Klux Klan. Forrest Gump was named for the old General, too. When Bob and Dottie had their first of four daughters, they named her Forrest, but not for the General. Dottie's mother's maiden name was Forrest.

In 1959, the KKK would pay Bob a visit and burn a cross in his yard in Birmingham for caring too much about racial brotherhood. After the "Karavan" of dozens of cars passed that night, Bob and about ten neighbors stood in a circle looking at the smoldering cross. A small boy asked Bob. "Was Jesus on that cross?" Bob's reply was, "In a way He was." The next day another neighborhood kid remarked how Jesus must have visited their house last night, because He left his cross in their yard!

Though his life has Forrest Gump parallels, Bob is no simpleton. History swings on tiny hinges and Bob and Dottie, like Forrest, have been on the scene of more than their share of turning points. After helping with the bus protest in Montgomery that launched the Civil Rights Movement, Bob started race relations groups across Alabama. That is why the Klan paid him a visit. He was sent to jail in Bessemer in 1960 because he would not be intimidated by a corrupt grand jury to hand over membership records of the Alabama Council on Human Relations.

The Methodist Church in North Alabama promptly rewarded his courage in standing up to the segregationists by kicking him out of the Conference. Some of his shocked fellow preachers got him reinstated just long enough to be sent to Southern Rhodesia (now Zimbabwe) as a missionary. Bob and Dottie went to Africa in early 1962 and were later kicked out by the racist colonial powers there who didn't appreciate his work for justice on behalf of the Mashona and Indebele tribes who were longing for freedom.

When he returned to America, Bob was hired by the US Justice Department as a crisis mediator. Bob served the Deep South out of Atlanta during the most turbulent years of racial integration in public schools. The day his friend Martin King was assassinated in Memphis in 1968 Bob went to mourn with King's Atlanta neighborhood that night.

In 1969, during a Poor People's March in Mississippi, Bob stood in the gap between the very nervous mayor of Yazoo City and the leader of the march as the police chambered their shotguns. His associate dove into a roadside ditch. But in anticipation of a bloody confrontation, Bob jumped into the street and hastily brokered a deal between the mayor and the marchers. They were allowed to pass through Yazoo City on their way to Jackson without bloodshed that day.

Bob and Dottie would move to Seattle, Washington to serve as a Justice Department mediator for the Northwestern Region and Alaska. This Alabama boy, usually working alone, was smack dab in the middle of Native American fishing disputes with White landowners. Bob also spearheaded responses to racist groups directing hatred toward ethnic minorities and the homosexual community in that area.

He was honored by the Birmingham Civil Rights Institute when it opened and still has a piece of the cross burned in his yard. Though recognized as a forerunner of God's Kingdom, he was never reinstated by the Methodist Church in Alabama or paid the pension he was due. Have you ever heard of Bob and Dottie Hughes? Few have. But in a Forrest Gump way, they have lived a life of devotion to Jesus and His Kingdom that has profoundly changed our world.

Proverbs 30:24-28 "Four things on earth are small, but they are exceedingly wise. The ants are a people not strong, yet they provide their food in the summer. The badgers are a people not mighty, yet they make their homes in the rocks. The locusts have no king, yet all of them march in rank. The lizard you can take in your hands, yet it is in kings' palaces."

If there *is* a "Forrest Gump anointing" in the Bible, it would be what author, Dutch Sheets calls, the "Lizard in Kings Palaces anointing" found in the above lines. Bob was literally a "lizard in Martin Luther King, Jr.'s palace."

A Lizard in the King's Palace

One of the stories my uncle recalled when I prodded him for memories of the old days was an event that took place in Montgomery, Alabama at Dr. Martin Luther King, Jr.'s church during the year of the Civil Rights Bus Boycott in 1955-56.

On this occasion, a Mass Meeting was called to walk the block and a half from the church to the Alabama Capitol steps for prayer. You have to visualize the scene. When you consider that the Confederate States of America was birthed right inside that Capitol building, leading to the Civil War, and that the spark of the Civil Rights movement was fueled in to flame by Martin Luther King, Jr. out of Dexter Avenue Baptist Church one block away and one century later, it is quite a spiritual epicenter.

As the mostly Black community gathered inside the church, a large mob of White people gathered outside. Perhaps the article about the upcoming event in the newspaper offended those in the

White community who saw their governmental shrine being desecrated by "niggers". It hurts me to write that word, but it was the word used by the voices of hate and this is the time to write about praying for enemies. The volatile crowd intended to block the path of those who would dare to walk over to the steps to pray.

My uncle and another White pastor in the Alabama Council for Human Relations were at the meeting inside the Dexter Avenue Baptist Church. They chose to go outside and stand at the front doors as a human shield. My uncle calls it a "ministry of presence." I call it "guts". Because the windows of the church were opaque, King's best friend, Ralph Abernathy would relay to others the scene Bob reported to him through the crack of the sanctuary doors. After what must have seemed like a very long time, something happened that my uncle describes as the single most courageous act he ever witnessed.

A lone black woman came out of the basement door and picked her way through the angry crowd over to the Capitol steps. Perhaps she wasn't attacked because she was just one person and posed no real threat to anyone in the mob, my uncle surmised. Bob watched in amazement as the woman emerged from the back of the crowd, walked over to the steps, and bowed her head in prayer. "Thus," Bob told me with a quivering voice at the power of the memory, "fulfilling the purpose of the day."

Someone then called in a fire alarm and fire trucks came screaming on the scene, dispersing the White crowd. It was a non-event relative to other unrest in that season. But for Bob, and now for me, the image of that unknown woman interceding for Alabama is an incurable wound for justice and racial healing in my soul. I dream the dream of Beloved Community in Alabama. I owe that woman something.

The Heart of an Intercessor

What is intercession and what is an intercessor?

Sometimes people only think of intercession as standing before God in verbal prayer on behalf of others. I can't tell you how true and important that image of an intercessor is. When we join the Cloud of

Witnesses it will blow our minds how human history turned on the hidden prayers of "Forrest Gump" saints. The role of intercession is not listed as a spiritual gift in Romans 12 or 1 Corinthians 12. Intercession is more than a gift; it is a *life*.

Jesus lived as an intercessor in everything He did. His cross was His way of standing in the gap between a world of lost humanity and the Father they broke covenant with. Listen to the writer of Hebrews:

In the days of his flesh, Jesus offered up prayers and supplications, with loud cries and tears to Him who was able to save Him from death and He was heard for His godly fear. Although He was a Son, He learned obedience through what He suffered; and being made perfect, He became the source of eternal salvation to all who obeyed Him. (Hebrews 5:7-9)

Jesus said in John 5:19, "*Truly, truly I say to you, the Son can do nothing of His own accord, but only what He sees the Father doing. For whatever He does, the Son does likewise.*" Not just His prayer life, but the whole of life for Jesus was intercession. It was engagement with life in real time that His Father used to teach Jesus what intercession was.

Because Jesus passed all the insanely difficult heart tests of this life, He is now our Great Intercessor in Heaven. He is eternally the God-Man. If there was ever a moment when He ceased to be fully God and fully Man we would lose our "anchor". The universe would fly apart! But there will never be a time when He will cease his intercession because His very being holds God and Men together. He crossed the impossible line between deity and humanity when He became flesh in Mary's virgin womb. He made God and Man one in His birth and sealed every promise in His death!

Therefore He is able to save completely those who come to God through Him, because He lives forevermore to intercede for us. (Hebrews 7:25)

We live in a universe that isn't anarchy because this one mediator and intercessor—Jesus, is sitting on the Throne of Heaven.

Intercession prepares the way for another ministry we inherit in Jesus – reconciliation.

Therefore, if anyone is in Christ, he is a new creation; the old has gone, the new has come! All this is from God, who reconciled us to Himself through Christ and gave us the ministry of reconciliation: that God was reconciling the world to Himself in Christ, not counting men's sins against them. And he has committed to us the message of reconciliation. We are therefore Christ's ambassadors, as though God were making His appeal through us. We implore you on Christ's behalf: Be reconciled to God. God made him who had no sin to be sin for us, so that in Him we might become the righteousness of God. (2 Corinthians 5:17-21)

To finish life well means we will all be intercessors and reconcilers at different times in different ways. It is who we *are* in Jesus. Intercession mercifully stands in the gap between parties. Reconciliation brings parties together.

My first big moment as an intercessor came when a snowball fight began between the Sigma Nu's and the fraternity next door at UNC-Chapel Hill. It was all fun and games until some of the guys started aiming for the windows of the houses. The sound of glass breaking on one side escalated into more glass breaking on the other. In a great act of insanity, I leapt up onto the wall separating the warring factions. At first I was successful in getting their attention to call for a cease fire.

My strategy to get them to stop gunning for the windows worked. But not in the way I thought. All of a sudden I became a far more interesting target than the buildings! I can't tell you how hard and fast college guys can wing snowballs. I have never seen so many projectiles coming my way...from both sides! Hey what are my dear fraternity brothers firing at ME for?! So much for my grand entrance into the world of peace negotiation! Lesson one for ministers of reconciliation – prepare to get clobbered!

Chapter 21

X Marks the Spot

"I looked for a man among them who would build up the wall and stand before me in the gap on behalf of the land so I would not have to destroy it, but I found none. So I will pour out my wrath on them and consume them with my fiery anger, bringing down on their own heads all they have done, declares the Sovereign Lord."
(Ezekiel 22:30-31)

Standing in the Gap

Standing in the "gap" as an intercessor is a big deal. If Moses were not willing to continually ask Yahweh for mercy, then Israel would have never made it to the banks of the Jordan River. God is searching for people to plead with Him for mercy, justice, and truth. Otherwise He has to come in judgment. He would *really* prefer not to do that.

God was merciful in 1956 to the people of Montgomery, of Alabama, of the US, and of the world because of intercession at Dexter Avenue's church door and on the Alabama State Capitol steps. A little piece of Jesus the Intercessor was in Bob as he stood in the gap between scared and angry Whites and Blacks. Everybody was scared and angry in Montgomery back then. A little piece of Jesus the Intercessor was also in that courageous Black woman as she stood in the gap between God and the government of Alabama.

In 1965, there would be a march for fair voting rights from Selma, Alabama to those same Capitol steps. It would come after horseback State Troopers beat marchers with clubs who had knelt to pray on Selma's Edmund Pettus Bridge. Though stopped on "Bloody Sunday", the march from Selma to Montgomery resumed after federal pressure forced Alabama's government to relent.

I wonder if the unknown woman who prayed and walked through her Red Sea of White people had anything to do with those who prayed and walked in 1965 to her same consecrated spot? Did she leave a spiritually radioactive "X" on the Alabama Capitol steps that marked that ground for every invisible angel and demon to see from then on? I really believe she did.

At the end of the Selma to Montgomery march, Dr. King would speak from the Alabama Capitol steps where Jefferson Davis gave his inaugural address as the Confederacy President a century before. King would say that day, "The arc of history is long, but it bends toward justice."

States Rights to Civil Rights to Kingdom Rights

The future belongs to intercessors. They are the ones agreeing with Heaven regardless of circumstances or opinions. They are the overlooked Forrest Gumps. Their names are forgotten or mocked by men, but written with eternal ink in God's book of remembrance. Sometimes prophetic intercessors gain national attention, but like John the Baptizer, Jesus the Suffering Servant, and Martin King Jr. the Drum Major for Justice, it is on their way to a martyr's death.

The fight for justice and righteousness in Alabama continues as I write this book. On September 1 of 2009, I was invited by Alabama Governor, Bob Riley, and his wife Patsy, to lead the weekly Tuesday 7am voluntary Bible study and prayer meeting that gathered in his office. Two dozen state servants from heads of banking, finance, and insurance departments, and their secretaries filled every seat around the board table and the chairs around the wall.

We looked at Isaiah 59:15-16, Hebrews 7:25, and Revelation 5:1-8 in order to see Jesus as the Great Intercessor between Heaven and Earth. I told the story of my uncle Bob standing as a human shield at Martin King's church just a block away in 1956. I pointed out the Capital window to where the woman prayed on the steps 53 years before. My Birmingham colleague that morning had the same name as another person who had stood on those Capital steps – Jeff Davis! After the Bible study I took pictures of my fellow minister, Jeffrey Davis, in front of the statue of Jefferson Davis, the Confederate President! There is a new generation of intercessors on the scene in Alabama!

Montgomery was the birthplace of the struggle for States Rights in 1861. It was the birthplace of the struggle for Civil Rights in 1955. The time has come for a fresh movement of Kingdom Rights in our day.

According to Romans 13:1, God delegates civil rights in this Age to the secular powers. "…for there is no authority except that which God has established. The authorities that exist have been established by God." In this Age the Church is a Kingdom of Priests. Followers of Jesus have positive and negative influence like salt and light, but there is no such thing as a Christian political state. "One Nation Under God" is a nice phrase describing a vision of America, but only the Praying Global Church fulfills that definition. The government of Heaven overrules all Earthly powers.

Politically, our world is in the midst of a global Human Rights movement. God desires that all governments be just and righteous. Justice and righteousness are the foundations of God's Throne. But in the Human Rights movement there is great debate as to whose definition of a right is right! The Human Rights movement, well intended as it may be, is not the final answer to human history. Man cannot save himself. We need a Savior. The good news is God has already sent Him.

In light of eternity, only God has "rights". Because, Jesus, as a Man, is the only One in human history who pleased God His entire life, He has an absolute right to be known, worshipped, and obeyed. He is the rightful leader of the Universe. The surrender terms of His coming Kingdom will be preached to every person before the end of this Age. His culture of true worship will contend with every culture of false worship. Shockingly, Human Rights and Kingdom Rights are in mortal conflict, because the real battle of history is about who deserves worship and who leads the future.

The stage is set for the final battle over the rights of the King to rule over His creation. The companion to this book, *Finishing History Well – Preparing for the Leadership of Jesus*, goes deeper on this subject. True and lasting justice is the leadership of Jesus, the Just One, on the earth.

Running With the Ball of Corporate Prayer in Stadiums

Like Forrest Gump running the football for Alabama's Crimson Tide in the movie, any praying saint who carries the ball of agreement with Jesus is the fastest one on the team. God is not looking for a superstar, He is looking for anyone who will agree with His heart of justice, righteousness, and truth.

One person agreeing with God's heart and helping our Nation do likewise is Lou Engle. Ending the innocent bloodshed of abortion drives Lou to call Solemn Assemblies of prayer and fasting in stadiums across America. Years ago Lou had a dream. He was digging for bones of justice. They all had "Alabama" written on them. Lou travels the nation re-digging wells of justice and revival based on the example of Isaac in Gen. 26:23. After Abraham, his father, had died, Isaac returned to the land where they had once pitched their tents. After re-digging the wells of his father, God came to Isaac in a dream and renewed the promises given to Abraham for his generation.

Lou knew there was a wellspring for justice and healing in Alabama. For years he would bring bus loads of young prayer warriors to pray and worship at key sites from the Civil Rights era. I first met Lou in September of 2003 *on the very spot* where my uncle Bob stood in front of the Dexter Avenue Baptist Church doors in 1956. Lou was a guest speaker for Lydia International, a women's intercessory prayer movement.

Neither Lou nor I had any idea that Lou would be back in Alabama again soon. He was preparing for a large prayer gathering at the Cotton Bowl in Dallas, Texas on November 29, 2003. He had chosen Dallas because it was the city from which the Roe vs. Wade case which legalized abortion had originated. It was also the city where President John F. Kennedy had been assassinated in 1963. Dallas was an important site from which the culture of death shrouding America had come. By gathering believers at key sites at key times, Lou re-digs wells of justice, healing, and revival around the country.

Pow-wow in Birmingham

Before the event in the Cotton Bowl, Lou had a word from the Lord that he must first walk in the shoes of the Native American and the African-American if he wanted to deal with the bitter root system of death beneath the abortion of millions of babies. He quickly organized a "Trail of Prayers" to pray and worship along Civil Rights sites and the Cherokee Trail of Tears. With three days notice, I organized hospitality for Lou and sixty of his young prayer warriors in downtown Birmingham.

President George W. Bush also came to the same block of 28th St in Birmingham on that same day, November 3, 2003. The black clad caravan of cars and Secret Servicemen came down the street in the morning for Bush to speak at a successful downtown business. Then, Lou and his buses of Kingdom dignitaries came just hours later to the dingy warehouse where we had set up a room for prayer and worship. That night a "pow-wow" of Native American leaders, African American leaders, Asian American leaders, and White guys like me met to hammer out some tough issues in the little warehouse prayer room.

Cherokee leader, Randy Woodley, gave a reluctant commendation of Lou to other Native leaders. That "one thumb up" from Randy paved the way for Cheyenne leader, Jay Swallow, to pray at the Cotton Bowl to reverse a curse of his great-great-grandfather. Cheyenne Chief, Black Kettle, watched US Cavalry troops, led by a Methodist minister turned colonel, massacre old men and pregnant women at Sand Creek in Colorado in 1864. Those killed at Sand Creek had rejected the call to bloody resistance from their warrior brethren and accepted the protection of the Colorado Territorial government. It was, like so many others, a treacherous betrayal of a signed covenant between Native Tribes and the United States government. God hates covenant breaking. It releases death.

Black Kettle survived and prayed that what had been done to his people would be visited upon the Americans. The accounts of the massacre, by the soldiers themselves, tell of cutting open bellies of pregnant women, hanging babies on tree limbs, and wearing wombs as skull caps. Indian children were used for target practice. This contempt for the elderly, women, children, the womb, and life itself released something very dark over America. Like our government today that slaughters infants in the womb through legal abortion, the government that had promised to protect Native People, ruthlessly slaughtered them. Sand Creek was one of the places where the bitter well of America's death culture was dug.

With no foreknowledge in the planning, "The Call – Texas" in the Cotton Bowl occurred on the *exact* 139th anniversary of the Sand Creek Massacre, November 29, 1864! Psalm 139 is where David says "you knit me together in my mother's womb, I am fearfully and wonderfully made." What a powerful example of reversing a curse over a nation. After The Call - Texas, a businessman gave money for much of the Sand Creek Massacre site to be given to the Cheyenne and Arapaho as a memorial. After years of additional gifts and purchases, that once tragic site is today a place of national redemption. The United Methodist Church repented for the actions of Colonel John Chivington, the Methodist preacher who led the massacre, by financially supporting the site restoration as well.

The Forrest Gump intercessors in Birmingham on November 3, 2003 were a part of opening windows in Heaven and wells on Earth for releasing justice. I would learn something later about November 3rd that made the little pow-wow in the Birmingham warehouse even more significant as a turning point for mercy. It would have to do with a baby boy named Max.

Valuing Life to the Max

Dale Cathey is the owner of the warehouse prayer room where the pow-wow took place. It has been a hidden Stairway to Heaven for the city of Birmingham since 1999. Dale and Jane had three sons. Two of them work with Dale in their home remodeling business. Let me tell you about Max. While Dale's wife Jane was carrying their third child, they learned their baby had a terminal birth defect. Their first doctor recommended an abortion. Dale and Jane came to a different conclusion from the doctor. Jane carried Max until a premature birth at seven months. Unable to survive apart from his mother, he died when the umbilical cord was cut. But Max was given a birthday.

The Birmingham News later carried the story of Dale and Jane's decision not to abort Max. After the article appeared, women and men who regretted their decisions for abortion began to call them both. Some women were grief stricken because they had given into the pressure or lack of support from the man involved. Men were also realizing that after taking care of the "problem" a deep burden of guilt and shame weighed upon them.

Are there soul wrenching thoughts going through the minds of men and women facing a pregnancy under adverse circumstances? Yes. Anyone who has ever been close to someone wrestling with the decision to abort knows it is overwhelming. Dale and Jane listened to a lot of pain during those phone calls. The amount of courage and support needed to move forward with a tough pregnancy seems beyond us. Even in ideal family situations, daily strength from God is needed when a crisis pregnancy is brought to birth. For all kinds of reasons some will choose abortion whether it is legal or not. But whether or not the decision is processed carefully, when an abortion is chosen, forgiveness from Jesus must come for full healing to begin.

Soon after Lou Engle came through Birmingham, I visited the Cathey's home and held Max's ashes. Max's certificate of birth and death was the same date as the warehouse pow-wow, November 3rd!

Was the decision of Dale and Jane not to slay an innocent child in the womb a part of reversing the curse of Chief Black Kettle following the innocent bloodshed of the Cheyenne? Was the whole chain of events mere coincidence? I can't prove it. But Romans 8:2 says, "Therefore, there is now no condemnation for those who are in Christ Jesus, because through Christ Jesus the law of the Spirit who gives life has set you free from the law of sin and death." This I do know for sure. The life giving Spirit of Jesus reverses the spirit of sin and death through all generations.

Jesus was the Great Intercessor of the November 3rd warehouse pow-wow. We who gathered that night really had no idea what we were doing other than meeting to reconcile differences. But in hindsight I see that our weak attempt to speak truth in love was a mysterious operation of the law of the Spirit of life reversing the law of sin and death. Something changed. God delights to use hidden acts of prayer and faith to change history. We may never know how a simple righteous choice changes eternity. But I am confident of this. Humble obedience by Forrest Gump intercessors become the spiritual "Xs" marking a new place of treasure that God uses to redeem time, people, and land.

God's Choice is Life

Dale and Jane chose to give birth to a son they knew would die. Dale has said many times that Max fulfilled his life's destiny on November 3rd, 1987. In a small way they made the same decision God made. Our Father chose to give birth to His Son knowing Jesus would die. Jesus fulfilled His life destiny dying for us. Choosing life, even when it means dying, brings more life.

For those who do not choose life, there is good news. God's choice for life will cover our choices for death. The blood of Jesus covers our sin. God wants to heal all our shame and guilt and has done so in His Son. Jesus' life was "aborted" on the cross. He became a bloody mess for all our bloody messes. What has been done to millions of babies in a bloody womb was done to Jesus on a bloody tree. Jesus' passion and death atones for the bloodguilt of all who participate in abortion, from our negligent culture to the doctor who kills the baby. We can all be forgiven, but we have to come to Jesus for it. No one else stood in our place as the intercessor clobbered for our choices. No other god or philosophy has the answer that Jesus has given us with His perfect blood.

Many women and men who choose abortion do so because of a lack of information, youthful immaturity, family or medical coercion, sins of self protection, or failing to recognize that their baby is known and loved by God. Sound counsel is vital. That is how crisis pregnancy centers serve our society. How will her decision affect her emotional and spiritual well-being for the rest of her life? How will her decision affect the destiny of the child she carries? Has she considered giving the baby to a family who will love and raise her child? What does the abortion procedure involve in terms of violence and pain to her and her baby?

Life is serious business. There are consequences to all our actions. Someone always pays for injustice. It may be us, it may be Jesus, it may be a stranger, or it may be a grandchild three generations later. But the God of the Bible, who allows the consequences of sin to go to the third or fourth generation, keeps His covenant of love for a thousand generations. (Exodus 20:5) There is judgment, but mercy exceedingly triumphs over judgment!

The CALL – ALABAMA

Lou Engle had the 7th Call event in Dallas in 2003 and then went more than three years before renewing another series of large prayer gatherings patterned after "solemn assemblies" described in the Old Testament book of Joel 2:15-17. Joel was a prophetic voice in his generation for Israel. Lou is doing for us what Joel did for Israel in calling a Nation back to the promises and blessings of God.

Blow the trumpet in Zion, declare a holy fast, call a sacred assembly. Gather the people, consecrate the assembly; bring together the elders, gather the children, those nursing at the breast. Let the bridegroom leave his room and the bride her chamber. Let the priests, who minister before the LORD, weep between the temple porch and the altar. Let them say, "Spare your people, O LORD. Do not make your inheritance an object of scorn, a byword among the nations. Why should they say among the peoples, "Where is their God?" (Joel 2:15-17)

The CALL – Nashville was held on 07/07/07 kicking off another series of mass meetings in the spirit of Joel 2 to cry out for God's mercy on a nation in crisis. On April 5, 2008, Lou came back to

Alabama to dig for more bones of justice and re-dig wells of revival. The Call – Alabama was a 12 hour fasting and prayer meeting in Montgomery spearheaded by the vision of local pastor, Kyle Searcy. It was a rainy morning but a few hundred brave wet marchers started at the Alabama Capitol Building steps to pray as we walked about a mile to the site of the prayer meeting where seven thousand others were gathering.

As we began our march, once again I thought of the unsung heroine of 1956 who prayed on those same Capitol steps. In 2008 we were marching and praying for another marginalized, voiceless people group in America - the unborn. As we moved down the steps to the street, Lou turned to me to help lead the march. But as we neared the Dexter Avenue Baptist Church, I began to break away from the marchers in the street. I ran up the steps to the spot in front of the balcony doors to the sanctuary where my uncle Bob had stood more than 50 years before. For me there was a "generational X of justice" marking that spot. I tossed down my umbrella, faced the church doors, and symbolically ripped them open. I wheeled around to raise my hands over the marchers and began to pray as the Spirit of God directed me. By standing on the same ground in the same spirit where Forrest Gump intercessors before me had stood, I became a part of continuing the spiritual legacy causing justice to "roll on like a river, righteousness like a never-failing stream!' (Amos 5:24)

X is Where the Treasure Lies

All the little pieces of sacred real estate today come from one spot of ground outside the gate of Jerusalem. Jesus' blood didn't just stain the dust near the city gate, it covers the world. God marked all creation as His treasure again when Jesus became an X on the cross. From where His X marks the spot, every curse is being reversed. It is the epicenter of the JUBILEE to come when the Justice of Jesus covers all the land, all the history, and all the people in His coming Kingdom.

Every good hero reflects God in some way. Jesus is the original Superman, Forrest Gump, and X-Man! Zorro may leave a Z, Jesus leaves an X! Our hearts are where His X marks the spot! We then become little X-Men who mark more hearts and places with our obedience and faith. As the global Body of Christ grows, God has more to work with all over the map. It is how we, as real life heroes of faith, prepare the world as a hot landing zone for Jesus' ultimate rescue operation. The Gospel of Jesus' Kingdom is the surrender terms offered us all before He comes to take charge of the planet. We surrender our rights for His rights. Alabama is one of those places on God's map that has a big ol' X on it. Jesus is a Treasure Hunter and we, along with *all* of Creation, are the treasure He is hunting.

Alabama may be the last state in many social categories, but we are the first state alphabetically! We are hanging on to that one! The name comes from a tribe in the Creek Indian confederation, the *Alabamos*, meaning "thicket clearer" or "path clearer". The name speaks of preparing the way. The forerunner spirit of John the Baptizer cleared the path for Jesus. As the birthplace for States Rights before the Civil War, and birthplace for Civil Rights before the Civil Rights Movement, we in Alabama are contending for God to birth a movement for Kingdom Rights! We want to be Kingdom Forerunners for Jesus' return!

On a map, X marks the spot where treasure lies. Hernando De Soto came as a treasure hunter to the Southeast of North America. Some of us Forrest Gump intercessors believe Alabama is where God buried a treasure, not of gold, but of justice. The flag of Alabama is a red St. Andrews cross, like an X, on a field of white. It is reminiscent of the Confederate battle flag, but it is nearly identical to the flag carried through Alabama in 1540 by Hernando De Soto, the Spanish Conquistador. I think of the verse in Isaiah 1:18 when I think of Alabama's colors:

"Though your sins are like scarlet, they shall be as white as snow; though they are red as crimson, they shall be like wool."

De Soto was a sinner and so were the Native Americans he came to. No one in Adam's race is completely good or completely bad. De Soto brought a lot of bad stuff to Native Americans when he came, but Indians love De Soto for one thing he brought North America—

the horse! Some of the Native tribes De Soto encountered were guilty of some really bad things. But the Timacua showed De Soto and his men how to barbeque the pigs the Spaniards brought. As sad as many things were about the first European and Native American encounters during the DeSoto expedition, the Indians got horses and the world got pork BBQ!

As long as there are people, good *and* bad things happen when we interact. It is what it is. In my short career as an intercessor and reconciler, I have realized we *never* dig completely through all the layers of past issues to the bottom of our clogged wellsprings. There is just too much emotional sediment. Then, while we are digging, more dirt keeps falling back into the well! At a certain point in the process of reconciling with others we simply have to let go of the past and start a new legacy. Others will NEVER know how much pain we bore and that has to be okay. Jesus drank the bitter cup to the very bottom. We have to let go of bitterness and give our pain and anger to the only One who can handle it. The cross is where all our sin must go for us to be saved from ourselves. Jesus the Great Intercessor and Reconciler has *already* borne the weight of the world so we don't have to.

"Make every effort to live in peace with everyone and to be holy; without holiness no one will see the Lord. See to it that no one falls short of the grace of God and that no bitter root grows up to cause trouble and defile many." (Hebrews 12:14-15)

To follow Jesus means we will choose to drink from the well-spring of His forgiveness and cease drinking from all of our bitter wellsprings of entitlement.

Back to the Cave Man

My friend Al Mathis owns DeSoto Caverns near Childersburg, Alabama. He calls himself a "cave man." Childersburg is the oldest continuously populated town in America; older than St. Augustine, Florida. Not only did De Soto come to the city of Chief Tuscaloosa's domain on the Coosa River in 1540, he likely visited the caverns nearby. One of the Spanish conquistadors became sick and stayed behind with a Negro Christian from the expedition. Childersburg has had black, white, and red men living there for more than 470 years! Like Joshua who brought Israel back to the Promised Land 470 years after Jacob left, in the heart of Alabama, in the womb of a cavern, X marks the spot where hidden promises of justice are being re-dug 470 years after De Soto.

Al didn't realize how insensitive to Native Americans it was for him to change the name of the caverns from Kymulga to DeSoto. De Soto is to Native Americans as Hitler is to Jews. "Kymulga" was a Chickasaw name meaning "Mulberries All" which was an idiom for "healing for all." Before then, the cave was called "Lam-hun-ga by the Muscogee Woodland Indians. That meant "Fathers out of the Hill." The caverns are inside a small mountain. The native peoples of the area believed the cave to be the womb from which they were birthed. The cave was the first cavern of record in American history. It was surveyed by the US Indian agent Benjamin Hawkins in 1796. During the period when General Andrew Jackson came through during the Creek War in 1813-14, Red Stick Creek Indians hid from him in the cave. Confederate soldiers made gunpowder from the bat guano during the Civil War. Over the last 35 years, Al turned the cavern into a successful tourist attraction and family fun park.

But the cave has in recent years been a prayer room made without human hands. Numerous Native American reconciliation gatherings have occurred there. Alabama Governor Bob Riley made a State Commendation honoring Samuel Checote, the Great Chief of the Muscogee Creek Nation in Oklahoma. Melba Checote Eads, Samuel's great-granddaughter, accepted the Governor's honor in the Cave on behalf of the Creek Nation on July 4, 2009.

Only weeks before this, Al discovered he was a relative of King Charles the 5th of Spain who commissioned De Soto's North American expedition from Barcelona. Al knew he was descended from the Royal Hapsburg family in Europe. Al's daughter, Joy, "just happened," to be on a college trip to Spain that got diverted from Madrid to Barcelona on July 3rd. Joy, also a Hapsburg, went down to the Barcelona docks where De Soto departed 470 years before. She wanted to pray from there for the reconciliation gathering in the cave at home. When she called her Dad, Al heard Native American flute music. Joy turned around the see Native Americans in full regalia singing on the Barcelona docks! God was up to some serious Transatlantic redemption!

Not only is Al descended from royalty in Europe, like me he is descended from family in Gadsden, Alabama. In fact, our ancestors are buried in the same cemetery there. One hundred years ago his grandparents from Gadsden got the crazy idea to buy the Kymulga Onyx Cave near Childersburg thinking the onyx could be mined for profit. God had His own plans for why the Mathis family would become the gatekeepers of a cave that carried a spirit for fathering and for healing for all. It may be for our grandchildren to search out more of the storyline of God on this tale. But I don't think it is an accident that the cemetery where our grandparents are buried is Forrest Cemetery! Even our forefathers and foremothers are Forrest Gump intercessors in the Cloud of Witnesses!

Al and I have become Forrest Gump, Caveman, X-Man, Treasure Hunter, Kingdom Forerunner intercessors! And the list is growing! For years now, have gone on crazy treasure hunting prayer journeys all over the map. Our wives are getting in on the adventure, too! Wanna come on our next trip? You don't have to. Just listen to the Holy Spirit and He will plan an amazing prayer itinerary for you... today! By following the leadership of Jesus we discover all kinds of treasures He has placed in the heart of the land and in the heart of the people. They are hidden in plain view. By prayer we go to where the X's are and we dig for treasures of justice in Jesus name to be released to a new generation. For those with eyes to see, the Xs are *everywhere*!

Finishing Life Well

Epilogue

"Do not be deceived: God cannot be mocked. A man reaps what he sows. Whoever sows to please their flesh, from the flesh will reap destruction; whoever sows to please the Spirit, from the Spirit will reap eternal life." (Galatians 6:7-8)

Dot, Dot, Dot - Life Goes On

What great HOPE is ours for finishing life well! Jesus did! Now He wants to live in us empowering us to do the same. The cross of Jesus means we, as flawed rebels, can begin again, no matter what we did last night. The good news is God's mercies are new every morning. If we don't quit, we win.

God sows His Spirit into the soil of all who say yes to Him. We are dirt with destiny! The Master Potter is shaping us all on His wheel to look like Him. Life is not our own, it is a gift. "You have been bought with a price, therefore honor God in your body." (1 Cor. 6:20)

We have promises from God in the Bible that enable us to live by faith during this Age of unbelief. Growing in our personal and corporate prayer life with God is how we weather every storm.

We live in a deeply broken world. Everyone is bent. Our cultural brokenness is evidenced by the wholesale breakdown of family and marriage relationships. Moral decline is hastening the day when America will become a second rate power. Her greatest resource has been her spiritual capital in God. That capital is far spent. A genuine spiritual awakening under the leadership of Jesus is our only hope.

The values of the Sermon on the Mount are there for all to see on the pages of Matthew's gospel. Living those realities *always* produce a culture God wants to bless. But will we together embody those values in the power of the Spirit of Jesus in a new generation? A great generation is one gripped by the wisdom of living for the Age to come enough to transform the generation we are in. My prayer is that our generation will be great.

Jesus our Great Intercessor and Reconciler is our example. Intercession and reconciliation as a lifestyle is what changes our world, one act at a time. Ten years after I was born again I first heard the voice of Jesus say, "Intercession is the pinnacle, Paul." I did not even know what the word *meant* at the time! We are all called to a life of prayer and action that releases the will of God on earth.

That is the challenge for us as I leave you, dear reader. Will we know Jesus intimately enough to be like Him in His greatness? Will we become the Forrest Gump generation of relentlessly foolish lovers our world so desperately needs to see? God is our treasure, our very great reward! The amazing thing is... we are Jesus' treasure, His very great reward! X marks the spot where treasure lies. Jesus has marked our hearts with His cross. Now we are global treasure hunters with Jesus. Let the adventure begin!

Will a City Finish Well?

Pray for me. A few years ago I told Jesus in the midst of a 27 hour Birmingham Prayer Furnace, "If You lead me, I will carry Birmingham in my heart."

I envision Jesus standing on Red Mountain above where the heart of Birmingham is nestled in Jones valley. My passion is for Birmingham to be the city of Jesus' dreams. A city transformed because God has healed the land and waters from all defiling injustices so that creation can participate with the redemption of the people. A city transformed because the Bridal People in this region understand who they are and the moment of history they have been given. A city with Kingdom blueprints built on the foundations of God's love through the government of a praying church.

Dr. King wrote a letter in 1963 from a Birmingham jail saying, "Injustice anywhere is a threat to justice everywhere." I believe it is time for a new letter to be written from out of Birmingham, Alabama with the converse of that message. "Justice anywhere is a threat to injustice everywhere." The Holy Spirit has whispered to me, "When Birmingham is transformed it will change Mecca." Wow. A transformed city anywhere can change cities everywhere. That thought drives me as I write the last book in the Finishing Well Series. Will a City Finish Well?

Those who have been forgiven much love much. Birmingham has been forgiven much. It is time for us to be dirt with destiny as the city-wide Bride of Christ. I know Jesus wants to marry me. But I also believe He wants to marry my city. What does *that* look like? I don't know. But night and day, city-wide, corporate prayer and worship, fueling night and day, city-wide corporate acts of justice and righteousness will be at the heart.

If Alabama is a Justice State, Birmingham is the Justice Gate. There is a wellspring of justice corked in the burning heart of the Bride of Jesus that is being re-dug by intercession and reconciliation in our city. When the wells of justice are uncorked and the treasures hidden in darkness are released from Heaven, the Bridegroom King will receive the worship that is rightfully His... and the world will quake.

The relay race of faith goes on. Are we running the final stretch of history before Jesus comes with a great shout?! That is the subject of *Finishing History Well*. But with our eyes fixed on Jesus we cannot lose! Let's press through to the end! By following the leadership of Jesus we *will* finish life well *and* prepare our generation for the leadership of Jesus when He returns!

Ministry Information

Paul Hughes is President of Kingdom Forerunners. Kingdom Forerunners was founded June 1, 2007 in Birmingham, Alabama as a Christian prayer leadership ministry.

paul@kingdomforerunners.com

The Purpose of Kingdom Forerunners is to prepare our generation for the leadership of Jesus by calling us to watch and pray, work for justice, and preach God's Kingdom. Kingdom Forerunners oversees numerous ministries including the Birmingham Prayer Furnace, Campus Prayer Networks, and Redigging the Wells.

Kingdomforerunners.com.

The Birmingham Prayer Furnace is a night and day, city-wide, house of prayer and worship that contends for the city of Jesus' dreams. Like the 24/7 iron blast furnaces in the Steel City of old, the Birmingham Prayer Furnace seeks for the fiery love of the Father to be poured in to the hearts of His children. Night and day, corporate worship and prayer fuels intimacy with Jesus, involvement in His mission, and calls the Bride of Christ in Metro Birmingham, Alabama to live with integrity and urgency until her Bridegroom King and Judge returns.

Birminghamprayerfurnace.com.

Redigging The Wells is a prayer movement for releasing justice in Jesus name to a new generation. Regional spiritual transformation involves healing generational wounds and renewing generational covenants to move cultures forward with biblical Kingdom values under the leadership of Jesus. Unified, corporate prayer at key places, with key people, at key times bring reconciliation, redemption, and transformation.

Rediggingthewells.org

Kingdom Forerunners Values

These biblical values undergird all of the ministries of Kingdom Forerunners.

1) Abiding in the Love of the Father
Abiding in the love of the Father is paramount to loving Jesus, loving the leadership of His Holy Spirit, loving His Word, loving His community, loving His mercy and justice, and loving His global Purpose.

2) Relationships and Healthy Community Rhythm Before Vision
We trust God to expand His work through a growing network of deepening friendships. We desire a stable core community that sustains healthy long term rhythms of work, worship, and rest. Corporate vision grows out of corporate Christ centered prayer, not a one man show.

3) Character Before Gifts
God values character, competence, and charisma, but growing Christ-like character shown by the fruit of the Spirit comes first.

4) Urgency of the Hour
The biblical signs of the times require our serious commitment to living as a generation prepared to see the return of the Lord. Understanding our climactic season in history is critical to the way we live

5) Openness to the Voice, Supernatural Gifts, and Leadership of the Holy Spirit

Jesus sent us the Holy Spirit to lead, teach, and empower us and He is quite able to do so. The Bride of Christ will increasingly radiate with trust in the leadership of Jesus as she walks in step with His Spirit during increasing global pressure.

6) Unity of the Sprit in the One Bride of Christ

Competition, jealousy, political maneuvering, gossip, and slander are from the dark side. The Bride of Christ transcends organizational, economic, ethnic, and cultural lines in any region. We must contend for the unity that Jesus purchased for us on the cross and learn to consider others better than ourselves through mutual submission.

7) Developing Prayer Friendly Cultures

The activity of group prayer involves the incorporation of various styles, philosophies, theologies, and practices that often conflict at a cultural and practical level. Leaders of corporate prayer gatherings need to become masters of discernment and cultural diplomacy in order to preserve the power of prayer across a city through agreement at the deepest heart level.

8) Counter-cultural Lifestyles of Simplicity, Gentleness, and Conviction

We cannot warn our generation if we live their worldly values system. The Sermon on the Mount culture and our willing response to live counter-cultural lifestyles now for a soon coming Kingdom is a privilege. Kingdom lifestyles go beyond personal piety and national politics to loving enemies and counting it joy to suffer for a gentle King of Kings who will one day crush all the other kings of the earth who oppose His leadership.

9) Multi-ethnic Ministry and Racial Justice

Birmingham as a city and Alabama as a state have a redemptive gift for releasing racial healing and justice to the earth. God has invited the Body of Christ in this area to walk out the dream of "Beloved Community" birthed in the Church of the Deep South in the 1950's for the sake of the healing of the Nations. The leadership core must understand and reflect this conviction.

Become a Ministry Partner of Kingdom Forerunners

The ministries of Kingdom Forerunners touch many lives through cultivating a Sermon on the Mount lifestyle of watching and praying, working for justice, and preaching God's Kingdom. Become a Kingdom Forerunner by joining the email list of one of the KF ministries. Donate to help build 24/7 prayer in Birmingham, grow movements of regional transformation, or fuel campus prayer networks. Participate in the prayer rooms, conferences, and ministry intensives that develop each year.

Order More Copies of The Finishing Well Series

Books in the Finishing Well Series may be ordered though any bookstore, through amazon.com, barnesandnoble.com, and google. com or through kingdomforerunners.com. These books are also available as ebooks through xulonpress.com. All proceeds from sales go into the non-profit ministries of Kingdom Forerunners.

CPSIA information can be obtained at www.ICGtesting.com
Printed in the USA
BVOW031201190812

297958BV00001B/6/P

9 781619 968103